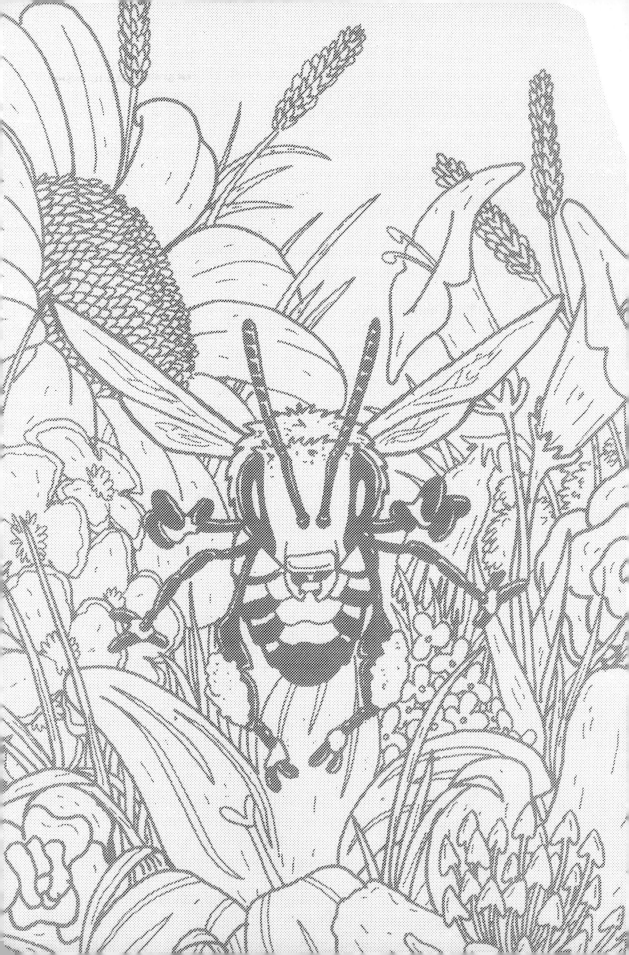

Jay Hosler, Ph.D.

*"We cannot win this battle to save species
and environments without forging an emotional
bond between ourselves and nature as
well--for we will not fight to save
what we do not love."*
--Stephen Jay Gould

For Max

FREE LIBRARY OF SPRINGFIELD TOWNSHIP

Also By Jay Hosler
The Sandwalk Adventures

Clan Apis

Third Printing

Printed in Canada

ISBN: 0-9677255-0-X

an Active Synapse production

Active Synapse
4258 North High Street
Columbus OH 43214-3048
Fax (614) 882-8470
www.ActiveSynapse.com
info@ActiveSynapse.com

Active Synapse
Probably Good For Your Brain!

Contents

Chapter One
TRANSITIONS

ONCE UPON A LONG,
LONG TIME AGO,
THERE WAS A
WHOLE LOT OF
NOTHING.

THE EMPTINESS WAS COMPLETE
AND IT PERSISTED STUBBORNLY
UNTIL IT DECIDED IT WAS TIME
FOR SOMETHING MORE.

AND THEN, SUDDENLY,
SOMETHING MORE
APPEARED.

A BUD. SMALL AND
DELICATE AND NESTLED
IN A CORNER OF THE
INFINITE VOID.

AND THERE IT WAITED.

AND WAITED.

AND WAITED.

AND WAITED UNTIL IT
HAD WAITED LONG
ENOUGH.

IT OPENED SLOWLY, SO THAT IT DIDN'T SHOCK THE EMPTINESS TOO MUCH.

THE PETALS STRETCHED INTO SPACE AND CAST THE ACHES OF DORMANCY OUT INTO THE DARKNESS.

THEY UNFURLED HESITANTLY, UNSURE OF HOW THE DARKNESS WOULD RECEIVE THEM. TO SHOW ITS APPRECIATION FOR THE OPPORTUNITY TO EXIST, THE WORLD FLOWER GAVE THREE GIFTS TO THE EMPTINESS.

IT BROUGHT LIGHT,

AND LIFE,

AND BEAUTY TO THE UNIVERSE.

AND THE EMPTINESS BEGGED FOR MORE.

PLEASED TO OBLIGE THE EMPTINESS, THE
WORLD FLOWER RELEASED A MIGHTY SWIRL
OF POLLEN GRAINS TO CARRY ITS GIFTS TO
THE FAR REACHES OF THE VOID.

EACH GRAIN
A DIFFERENT SIZE
AND SHAPE THAN
THE NEXT.

SOME WERE
HOT AND FIERY.

SOME WERE
ICY COLD.

STILL OTHERS WORE
AMAZING ORNAMENTAL
RINGS AND BAUBLES.

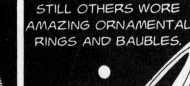

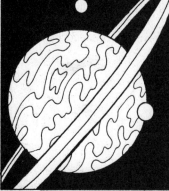

AND SOME VERY SPECIAL
GRAINS WERE COVERED IN
SLOSHING BLUE OCEANS
AND FERTILE LANDS.

ON THESE SPECIAL
GRAINS, LIFE COULD
GROW.

IT FIRST GREW IN THE SEAS; BIT BY BIT, CHUNK BY CHUNK, A FEW MOLECULES HERE, A FEW MOLECULES THERE.

EVENTUALLY, WHEN IT GOT THE KNACK OF PUTTING ITSELF TOGETHER, *LIFE* EXPLODED INTO BRAIN-BENDING DIVERSITY.

THE OCEANS SWARMED WITH GOBS AND GOBS OF PLANTS, PREDATORS AND PREY. IT WAS A PRETTY EXCITING TIME.

LIFE WAS A SMASHING SUCCESS. IT WAS EVERYWHERE, AND SOON THE OCEANS GREW CRAMPED.

OUCH!

EXCUSE ME.

WATCH IT!

QUIT POKING ME!

HEY, THAT TICKLES!

WHO STINKS?

ONE DAY, A BRAVE LITTLE AMPHIBIOUS THING, DESPERATE FOR SOME ELBOW ROOM, DECIDED TO CRAWL OUT ONTO THE LAND.

SHE THOUGHT SHE WAS THE FIRST BOLD PIONEER INTO THIS STRANGE NEW WORLD.

SHE WASN'T.

WELL, WELL, WELL.

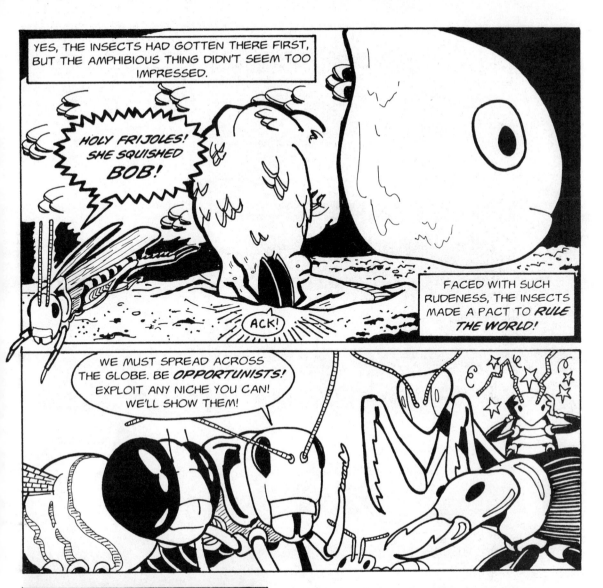

YES, THE INSECTS HAD GOTTEN THERE FIRST, BUT THE AMPHIBIOUS THING DIDN'T SEEM TOO IMPRESSED.

HOLY FRIJOLES! SHE SQUISHED *BOB*!

ACK!

FACED WITH SUCH RUDENESS, THE INSECTS MADE A PACT TO *RULE THE WORLD*!

WE MUST SPREAD ACROSS THE GLOBE. BE *OPPORTUNISTS*! EXPLOIT ANY NICHE YOU CAN! WE'LL SHOW THEM!

THEIR PLAN WORKED. EVENTUALLY, THE INSECTS COMPRISED OVER HALF OF ALL THE ANIMALS ON THE PLANET.

THEY WERE A DIVERSE GROUP. MOST WERE SOLITARY, BUT A FEW FOUND THAT THEY HAD BETTER SUCCESS SURVIVING IF THEY WORKED TOGETHER.

AMONG THESE SOCIAL INSECTS, THERE WAS ONE CLAN THAT CARED FOR THE CHILDREN OF THE WORLD FLOWER IN EXCHANGE FOR NECTAR AND POLLEN.

THIS IS THE STORY OF THAT CLAN OF HONEY BEES.

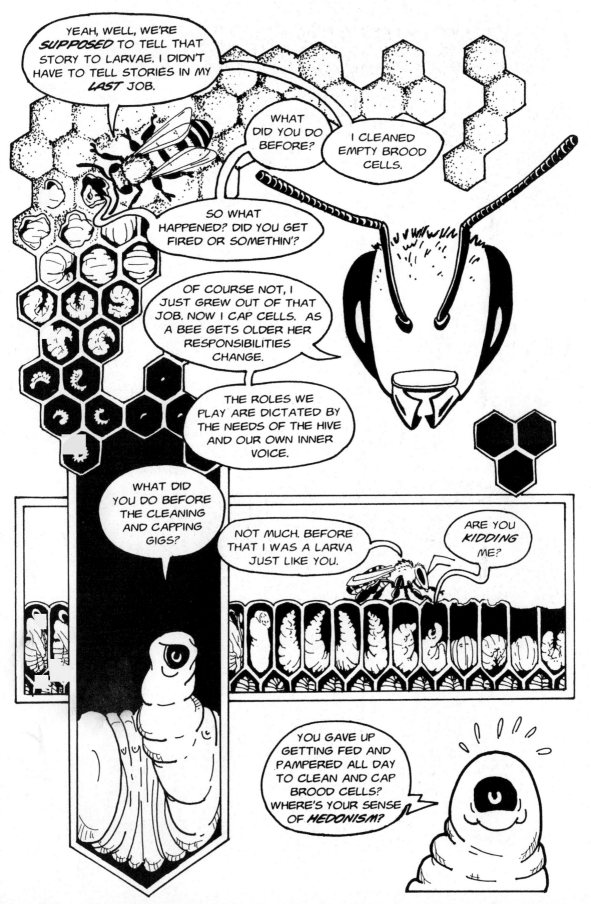

19

20

ALL I WANT TO DO IS SIT HERE AND EAT.

ARE YOU HUNGRY RIGHT NOW?

NO.

AND DO YOU KNOW WHY? YOUR WEIGHT HAS INCREASED *2000 TIMES* IN YOUR FIVE DAYS AS A LARVA. YOU'VE BEEN EATING SO MUCH FOOD SO THAT YOUR BODY HAS THE ENERGY FOR THE METAMORPHOSIS. THE FACT THAT YOU'RE *NOT* HUNGRY ANYMORE MEANS YOUR BODY IS READY FOR THE CHANGE.

PLEASE DON'T MAKE ME DO THIS, DVORAH.

YOU HAVE TO.

WHY?

BECAUSE YOU *DO.*

BUT *WHY?*

OK, OK, I'M *SORRY.*

BECAUSE I'M YOUR OLDER SISTER AND *I SAID SO!*

NOW QUIT PESTERING ME AND LET ME FINISH MY WORK.

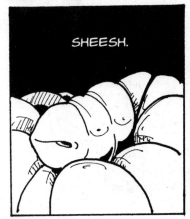

SHEESH.

I'M GONNA NEED A MANUAL OR SOMETHING, Y'KNOW.

22

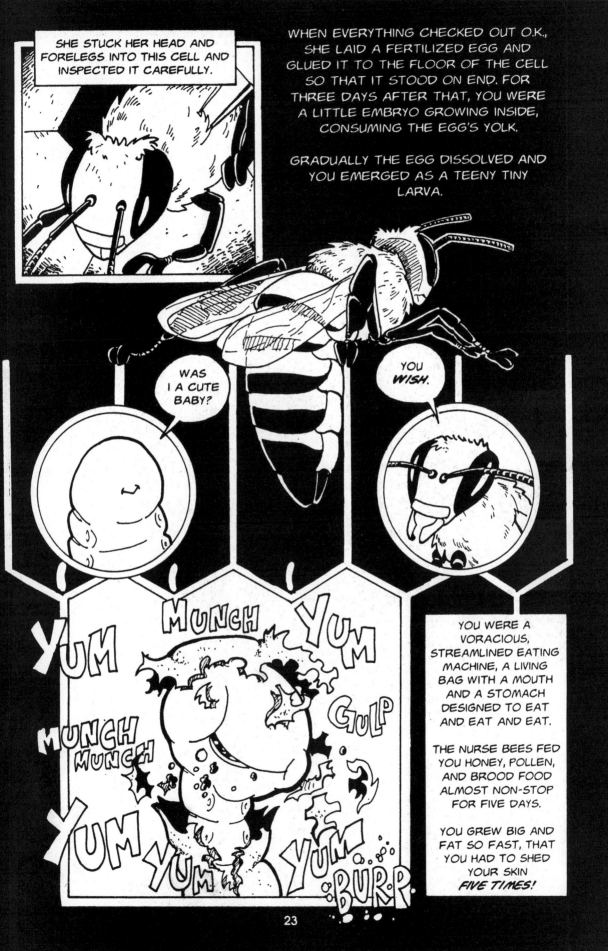

SHE STUCK HER HEAD AND FORELEGS INTO THIS CELL AND INSPECTED IT CAREFULLY.

WHEN EVERYTHING CHECKED OUT O.K., SHE LAID A FERTILIZED EGG AND GLUED IT TO THE FLOOR OF THE CELL SO THAT IT STOOD ON END. FOR THREE DAYS AFTER THAT, YOU WERE A LITTLE EMBRYO GROWING INSIDE, CONSUMING THE EGG'S YOLK.

GRADUALLY THE EGG DISSOLVED AND YOU EMERGED AS A TEENY TINY LARVA.

WAS I A CUTE BABY?

YOU *WISH.*

YUM MUNCH YUM GULP MUNCH MUNCH YUM YUM YUM BURP.

YOU WERE A VORACIOUS, STREAMLINED EATING MACHINE, A LIVING BAG WITH A MOUTH AND A STOMACH DESIGNED TO EAT AND EAT AND EAT.

THE NURSE BEES FED YOU HONEY, POLLEN, AND BROOD FOOD ALMOST NON-STOP FOR FIVE DAYS.

YOU GREW BIG AND FAT SO FAST, THAT YOU HAD TO SHED YOUR SKIN *FIVE TIMES!*

23

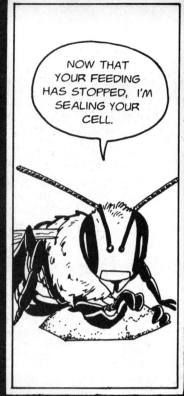

NOW THAT YOUR FEEDING HAS STOPPED, I'M SEALING YOUR CELL.

WHEN I'M DONE, YOU'LL ORIENT YOUR HEAD TO THE CAPPED END OF THE CELL, STRETCH OUT AND BEGIN THE CONSTRUCTION OF YOUR COCOON.

THWIP!

AND *WHEN* DO I GET THE MATERIALS TO BUILD *THAT*?

YOU ALREADY HAVE THEM. YOU WEAVE THE COCOON WITH SILK FROM THE *SPINNERETS* IN YOUR MOUTH.

WOW. THAT IS SO *COOL*.

"WELL, SORTA. EARLY IN THE CONSTRUCTION PROCESS, YOU'LL EXCRETE THE WASTE MATERIAL THAT HAS BUILT UP DURING YOUR FIVE DAY EATING BINGE. YOU'LL USE THE FECES TO SUPPLEMENT THE SILK IN THE CONSTRUCTION OF THE COCOON."

OH, COME *ON*. NOW YOU'RE JUST TRYING TO GROSS ME OUT.

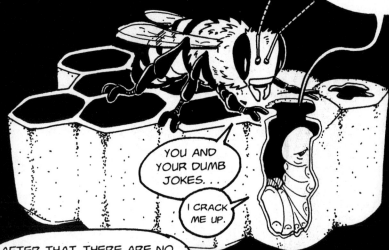

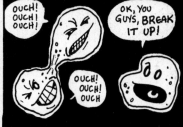

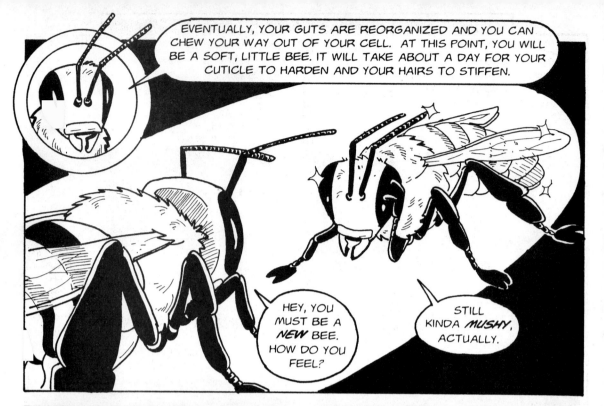

EVENTUALLY, YOUR GUTS ARE REORGANIZED AND YOU CAN CHEW YOUR WAY OUT OF YOUR CELL. AT THIS POINT, YOU WILL BE A SOFT, LITTLE BEE. IT WILL TAKE ABOUT A DAY FOR YOUR CUTICLE TO HARDEN AND YOUR HAIRS TO STIFFEN.

HEY, YOU MUST BE A *NEW* BEE. HOW DO YOU FEEL?

STILL KINDA *MUSHY*, ACTUALLY.

ON TOP OF THAT, YOUR INSIDES WON'T BE COMPLETELY DONE DEVELOPING. MAKE SURE YOU EAT A LOT OF POLLEN AS SOON AS YOU EMERGE SO THAT YOUR MANDIBULAR GLANDS AND FAT BODIES FORM PROPERLY.

Gobble Gobble Gool Gobble

AND THAT'S WHAT HAPPENS DURING METAMOPHOSIS

I SEE.

27

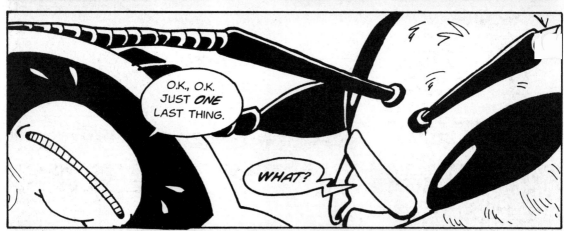

28

BELIEVE ME, LITTLE SISTER, THERE IS NOTHING TO FEAR. WHAT IS ABOUT TO HAPPEN MAY SEEM STRANGE, BUT IT IS PERFECTLY NATURAL.

AND WHEN IT'S ALL DONE, I'LL BE HERE WAITING FOR YOU.

I PROMISE.

BUT I FEEL SO ISOLATED, DVORAH.

I FEEL SO *ALONE.*

I KNOW.

I ONCE FELT THE SAME WAY.

UNFORTUNATELY, WHAT YOU HAVE TO DO NOW, YOU HAVE TO DO ALONE.

BUT TRUST ME, NYUKI. WHEN THIS IS ALL OVER AND YOU CRAWL OUT OF THIS LITTLE CELL. . .

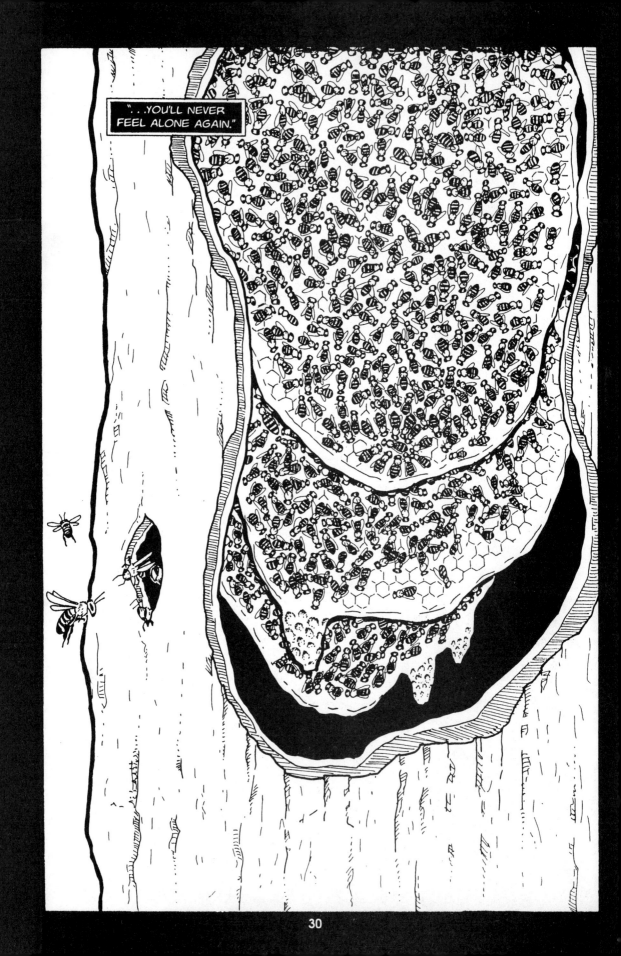

"...YOU'LL NEVER FEEL ALONE AGAIN."

Chapter Two
SWARM

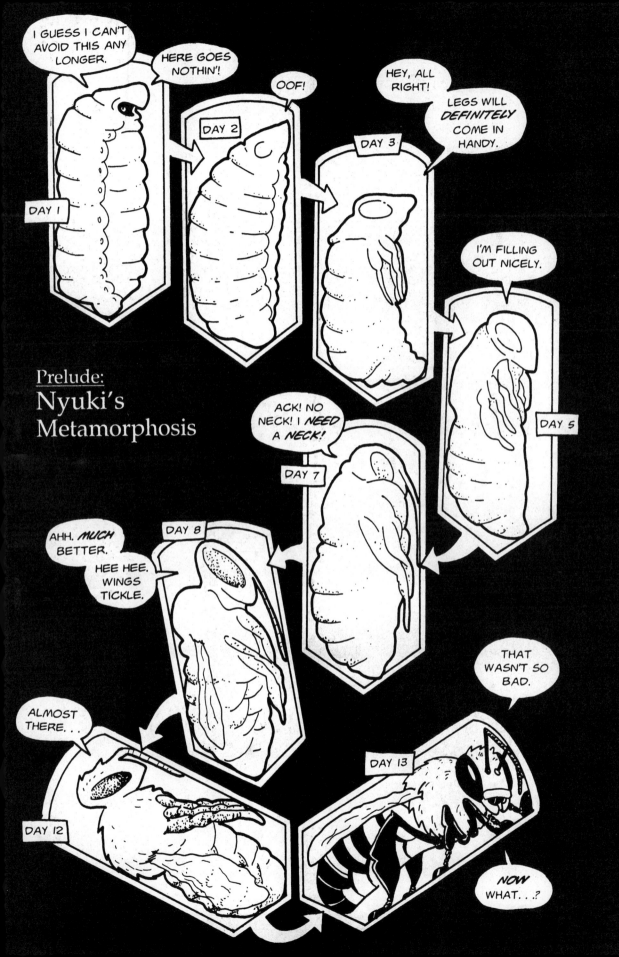

CHAPTER TWO: SWARM

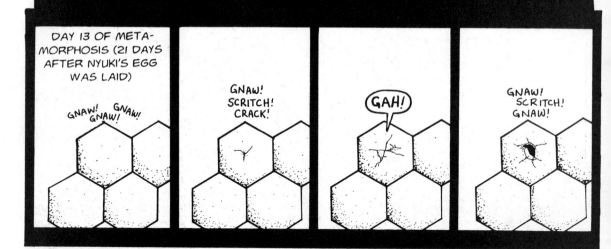

WELL, THAT MAY BE, BUT THE *EGG* I HATCHED FROM WAS LAID BY THE QUEEN *HERSELF.*

WELL, DUH. THE QUEEN'S THE ONLY BEE THAT MATES. SHE LAYS *ALL* THE EGGS IN THE HIVE.

GEE-WHIZ. I THOUGHT I WAS SPECIAL.

OH, YOU'RE *SPECIAL* ALL RIGHT.

YOU'RE THE *BIGGEST* GOOFBALL I'VE *EVER* MET.

HA HA HA.

SIGH.

YOU'RE MAKING FRIENDS FAST, NYUKI.

DVORAH?

36

SORRY. I JUST STARTED WORKING *VENTILATION*. IT'S MY FIRST JOB OUTSIDE THE HIVE AND I'M KINDA TENSE.

THE HIVE HAS BEEN WARMER THAN USUAL AND MANY OF US HAVE BEEN RECRUITED TO COOL IT DOWN.

NURSE BEES PLACE DROPS OF WATER THROUGHOUT THE HONEYCOMB....

...WHILE WE VENTILATORS FACE THE MOUTH OF THE HIVE WITH OUR ABDOMENS DOWN AND BEAT OUR WINGS.

THIS DRAWS THE STUFFY AIR OUT OF THE HIVE AND EVAPORATES THE WATER.

WHAT A *CHILLING* STORY! HEE HEE.

UGH. I'D FORGOTTEN ABOUT YOUR ROTTEN JOKES.

THAT'S JUST WHAT THIS HIVE NEEDS:

MORE HOT AIR.

WELL, THANKS, I LIKE TO. . . *HEY!*

DID YOU COME INSIDE JUST TO GIVE ME A HARD TIME?

SORTA. ABOUT 30% OF EVERY BEE'S DAY IS SPENT RESTING. I THOUGHT I'D SPEND MY BREAK MAKING SURE YOU GET SITUATED.

HERE'S WHERE WE KEEP THE POLLEN.

DIG IN.

MUNCH MUNCH. *MMMM.* THIS REALLY HITS THE SPOT.

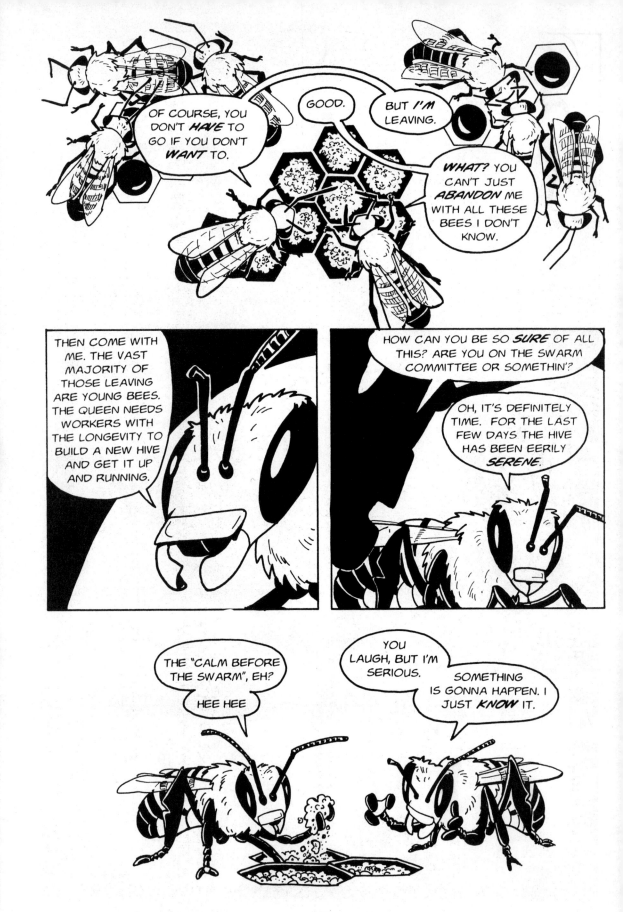

40

YEAH, YEAH. THIS IS STARTING TO SOUND LIKE ONE OF YOUR GOOFY FAIRY TALES, DVORAH.

REMEMBER THE ONE YOU TOLD ME ABOUT THE "WORLD FLOWER"?

GIMME A BREAK.

GRRR.

LOOK, I DON'T CARE IF YOU BELIEVE ME OR NOT. I'M TELLING YOU, SOME-THING IS GOING TO -

OOF!

GANGWAY!

THE TIME IS NEAR!

GET EXCITED!

SWARM!

SWARM!

SWARM!

WOW. THEY'RE GOIN' NUTS!

WHO'S THAT BIG, FAT BEE THEY'RE ALL PUSHING AROUND, DVORAH?

GREAT GOOGALY MOOGALY!

THAT'S QUEEN HACHI!

41

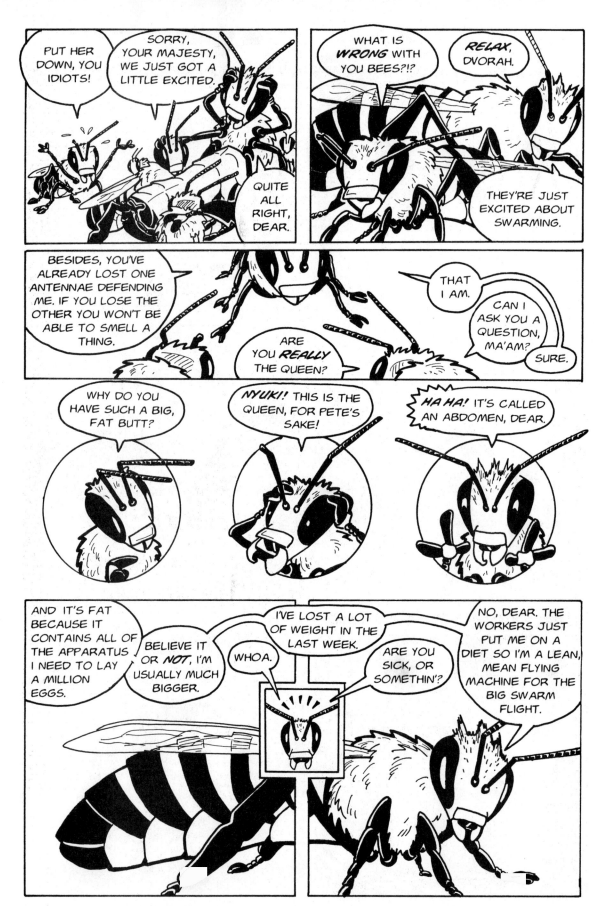

WAIT A MOMENT. DID YOU CALL HER *NYUKI*?

IS THIS THE *SPECIAL* LITTLE SISTER YOU TALKED ABOUT SO MUCH WHEN YOU WERE ONE OF MY ATTENDANTS, DVORAH?

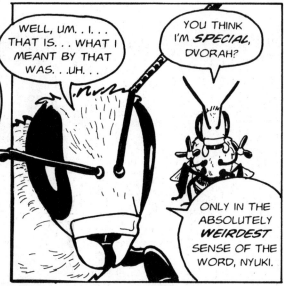

WELL, UM. . . I. . . THAT IS. . . WHAT I MEANT BY THAT WAS. . .UH. . .

YOU THINK I'M *SPECIAL*, DVORAH?

ONLY IN THE ABSOLUTELY *WEIRDEST* SENSE OF THE WORD, NYUKI.

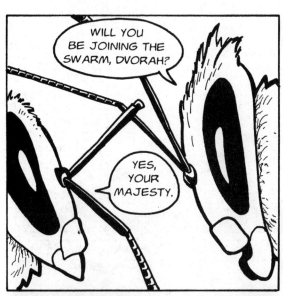

WILL YOU BE JOINING THE SWARM, DVORAH?

YES, YOUR MAJESTY.

EXCELLENT. AND YOU NYUKI?

WELL, I'M NOT SO *SURE*. . .

VERY WELL. BUT YOU MUST DECIDE SOON. THE NEW QUEENS ARE ALMOST READY TO EMERGE.

Y'KNOW, I JUST DON'T UNDERSTAND *ANY* OF THIS.

IF WE ALREADY *HAVE* A QUEEN, WHY WOULD THE HIVE RAISE MORE?

WELL, IT'S A COMPLICATED CONVERGENCE OF SEVERAL FACTORS, NYUKI.

YOU SEE, THE QUEEN OF A HIVE IS BOTH *SLAVE* AND *SOVEREIGN*.

AS SLAVE, I AM CONTINUOUSLY LAYING EGGS TO GENERATE MORE WORKERS FOR THE HIVE.

HUP, 2, 3, 4

HUP, 2, 3, 4

WHEW!

PICK-UP THE PACE, QUEENIE.

BUT AS SOVEREIGN, I CONTROL THE WORKERS WITH CHEMICALS I RELEASE FROM MY BODY CALLED *PHEROMONES*.

MY ATTENDANTS CARRY THESE PHEROMONES FROM ME TO WORKERS ALL OVER THE HIVE.

QUEENS ARE MADE WHEN WORKERS FEED A NORMAL LARVA A WHOLE BUNCH OF ROYAL JELLY. WHEN EXPOSED TO MY PHEROMONES, WORKERS LOSE THEIR DESIRE TO DO THIS.

HEY, *I* HAVE AN IDEA.

LET'S *NOT* RAISE ANY NEW QUEENS.

OOO. I *LIKE* THE WAY YOU THINK.

NTUALLY, AS MORE AND MORE ORKERS ARE BORN, THE HIVE BECOMES OVERCROWDED.

WITH THE HIVE SO CONGESTED, THE EFFECTS OF MY PHEROMONES ARE DILUTED BECAUSE MY ATTENDANTS CAN'T GET THE PHEROMONES TO ALL THE WORKERS. CONSEQUENTLY, I LOSE CONTROL AND WORKERS START REARING NEW QUEENS.

HEY, I HAVE AN IDEA.

LET'S RAISE SOME *NEW* QUEENS.

OOO. I *LIKE* THE WAY YOU THINK.

WHICH IS JUST AS WELL, SINCE THE HIVE WILL NEED A NEW QUEEN ONCE HALF THE COLONY AND I SWARM TO RELIEVE THE OVERCROWDING.

.T'S ALL PART OF THE NATURAL CYCLE OF THE HIVE, NYUKI.

BZZT BZZT

FREEZE.

DO YOU HEAR THAT?

BZZZZT BZ

46

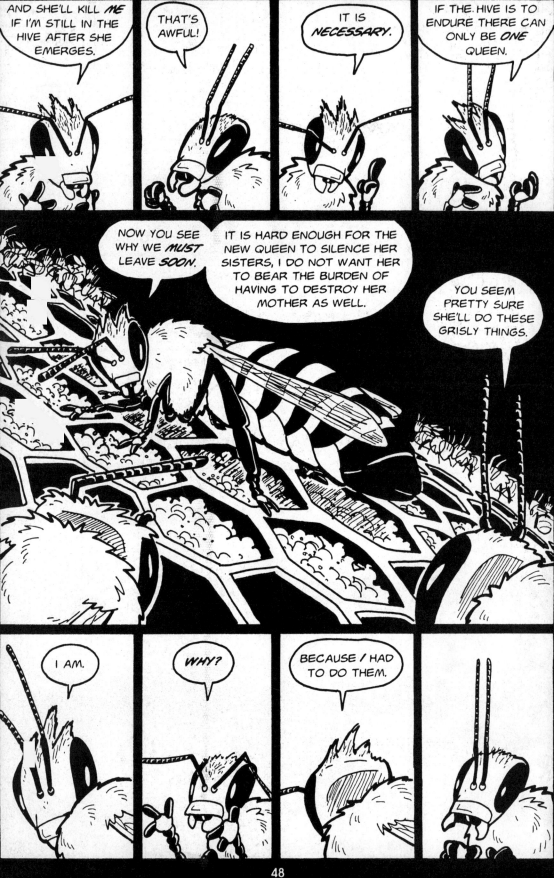

AND SHE'LL KILL *ME* IF I'M STILL IN THE HIVE AFTER SHE EMERGES.

THAT'S AWFUL!

IT IS *NECESSARY.*

IF THE HIVE IS TO ENDURE THERE CAN ONLY BE *ONE* QUEEN.

NOW YOU SEE WHY WE *MUST* LEAVE *SOON.*

IT IS HARD ENOUGH FOR THE NEW QUEEN TO SILENCE HER SISTERS, I DO NOT WANT HER TO BEAR THE BURDEN OF HAVING TO DESTROY HER MOTHER AS WELL.

YOU SEEM PRETTY SURE SHE'LL DO THESE GRISLY THINGS.

I AM.

WHY?

BECAUSE *I* HAD TO DO THEM.

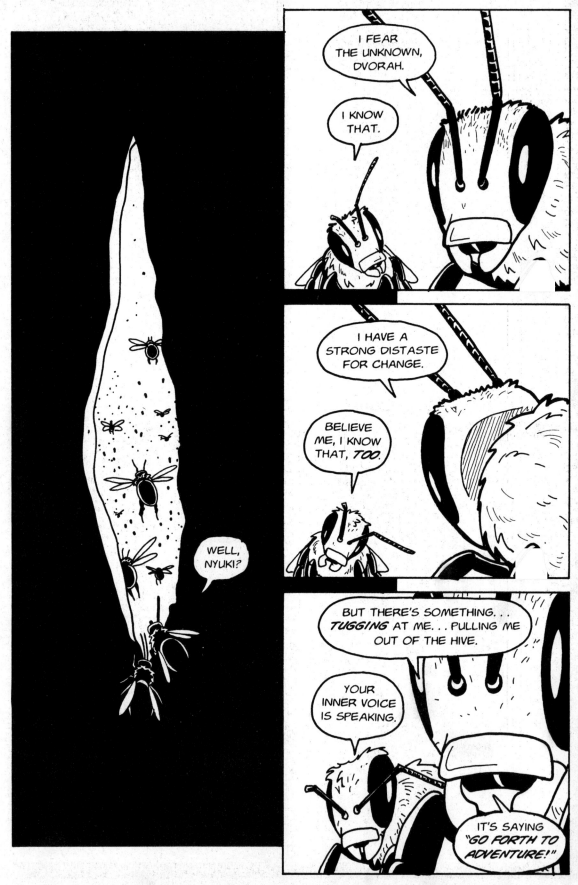

50

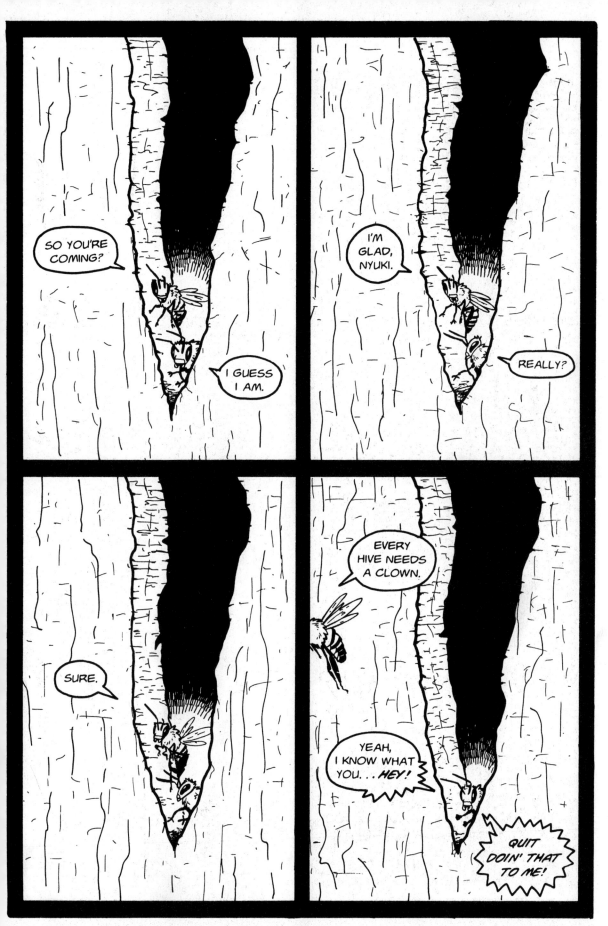

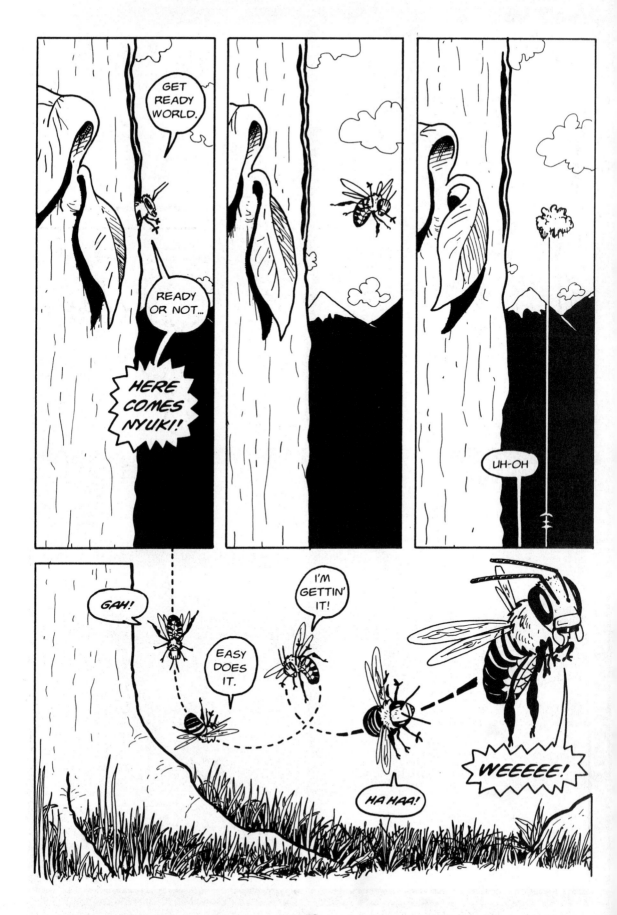

SO YOU'RE COMING?
I GUESS I AM.
I'M GLAD, NYUKI.
REALLY?
SURE.
EVERY HIVE NEEDS A CLOWN.
YEAH, I KNOW WHAT YOU. . . HEY!
QUIT DOIN' THAT TO ME!

52

OK, LISTEN UP, EVERYBODY!

WE NEED SCOUTS TO GO OUT AND FIND A SUITABLE SITE FOR A NEW NEST.

I CAN DO IT!

I'LL GO!

ME TOO!

I'M JOINING THE SEARCH, NYUKI.

YOU BETTER STAY WITH THE CLUSTER SINCE YOU'RE STILL YOUNG AND INEXPERIENCED.

BUT, FLYING IS SO MUCH *FUN*. I WANT TO GO, TOO.

NO. JUST SIT TIGHT.

AND, STAY OUT OF TROUBLE.

I'LL BE BACK IN A BIT.

54

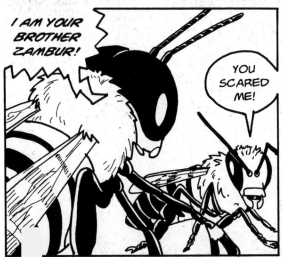

AH, YES. SOON THE SCOUT BEES WILL RETURN WITH MANY POSSIBLE NEST SITES. THEN EACH WILL DO A DANCE THAT POINTS IN THE DIRECTION OF THE NEST SITE THEY HAVE FOUND.

THE BETTER THE NEST SITE, THE MORE EXCITING THE DANCE. EVENTUALLY WE SHALL ALL ATTEND TO THE SCOUT WITH THE BEST DANCE AND FOLLOW HER TO THE NEW NEST.

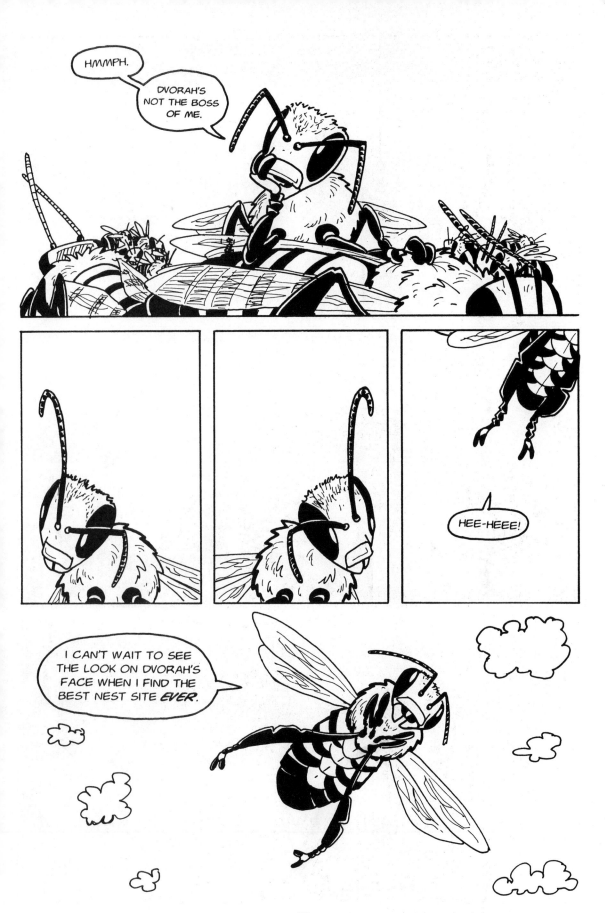

WOW! LOOK AT *THAT* ONE!

BIG SOLID TREE.

ROOMY INTERIOR.

AND LOTS OF FLOWERS AROUND.

HOT DIGGETY! I CAN'T WAIT TO TELL THE OTHERS!

Chapter Three
HIDE & SEEK

HELLOO? WHO'S IN THERE?

UM --- NOBODY.

HA HA. THERE'S NO NEED TO BE SHY. COME ON OUT.

I'M NOT SHY.

I'M HUNGRY.

WOW. YOU BLEND RIGHT IN WITH THE LEAVES.

YES. IT MAKES IT EASIER TO *HIDE.*

OH, I'M SORRY. I'VE DISTURBED YOU.

NO. NO. I WAS JUST GETTING READY TO EAT.

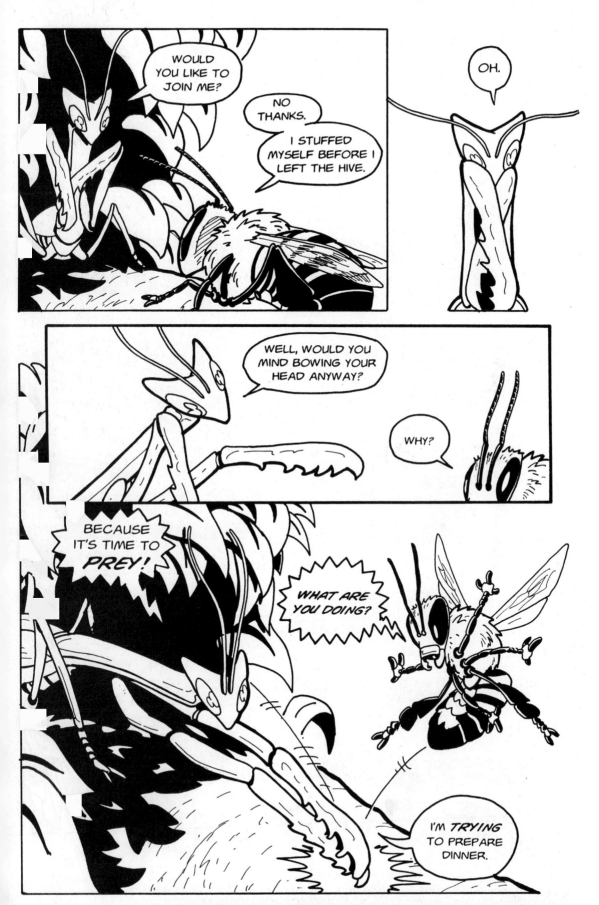

65

71

SISYPHUS! YOU BUMBLING BEETLE!

YOU HIT MY FLOWER AND MY FOOD GOT AWAY!

IT WAS AN ACCIDENT, THOM.

MY VISIBILITY IS A BIT HAMPERED SINCE I'M WALKING BACKWARDS, Y'KNOW.

BUT I AM HUNGRY!

PATIENCE IS THE PRICE OF AN AMBUSH STRATEGY, THOM.

BESIDES, HOW COULD YOUR FOOD GET AWAY? I THOUGHT YOUR PREY DIED INSTANTANEOUSLY WHEN YOU CRAB SPIDERS BITE THEM.

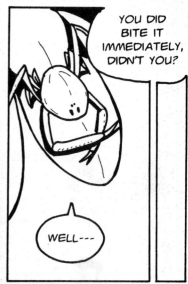

YOU DID BITE IT IMMEDIATELY, DIDN'T YOU?

WELL---

THOM, THOM, THOM.

WERE YOU GLOATING AGAIN?

NONE OF YOUR BUSINESS! JUST WATCH WHERE YOU'RE GOING FROM NOW ON!

Y'KNOW, EVERY TIME I TALK TO THAT GUY I'M REMINDED OF WHY THEY'RE CALLED CRAB SPIDERS.

WHAT A GROUCH.

74

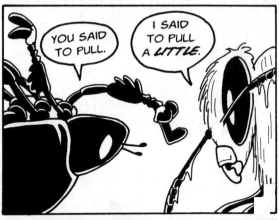

77

WELL, NYUKI, IT JUST SO HAPPENS THAT I PASSED YOUR SWARM BEFORE WE "BUMPED" INTO EACH OTHER.

THEN YOU CAN TAKE ME? I'M NOT GONNA DIE?

THERE ARE NO GUARANTEES IN THIS WORLD, DEAR GIRL. BUT, AS LONG AS YOU DON'T HAVE ANOTHER MELODRAMATIC HISSY FIT, *I* PROMISE NOT TO KILL YOU.

DEAL.

GOOD.

LET ME GET MY BALL AND WE'LL BE OFF.

WHAT IS THIS THING?

DUNG.

POOP?

YEP. I'M A DUNG BEETLE. WE COLLECT COW DUNG AND FEED IT TO OUR LARVA.

YUCK!

HMMP. IT'S NO MORE UNPALATABLE THAN HONEY.

YOU SURE *SEEM* TOUCHY.

WELL MAYBE THAT'S BECAUSE EVERYONE I'VE MET SINCE I LEFT THE HIVE IS NOTHING LIKE ME. YOU'RE ALL SO---WEIRD.

THAT'S A MATTER OF PERSPECTIVE.

MOST LIVING THINGS LIVE ALONE AND FEND FOR THEMSELVES. HONEY BEES ARE A *RARE* EXAMPLE OF ANIMALS THAT LIVE AND WORK TOGETHER FOR THEIR MUTUAL BENEFIT. YOUR SOCIAL BEHAVIOR MAKES *YOU* THE WEIRDOS IN THE ANIMAL KINGDOM, NOT US.

I LIKE TO THINK THAT IT MAKES US *SPECIAL*.

AS I SAID, IT'S ALL A MATTER OF PERSPECTIVE.

I GUESS.

UH OH.

WHAT?

QUICK, GET UNDER THE DUNG!

WOW. THERE'S SOMETHING YOU DON'T HEAR EVERY DAY.

IF I STING I DIE?

COULD YOU *ELABORATE* ON THAT?

SURE.

YOUR STING HAS BARBS ON IT.

IF YOU STUNG THAT BIRD...

...THE BARBS WOULD GET STUCK IN ITS ELASTIC SKIN...

...AND THE STING WOULD GET PULLED OUT OF YOUR BODY ALONG WITH SOME OF YOUR GUTS WHEN YOU TRIED TO GET AWAY.

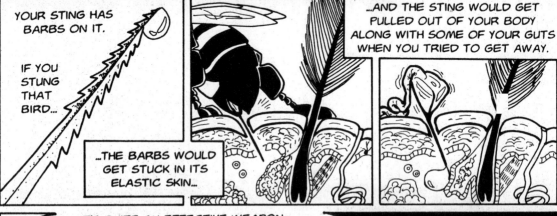

IT'S QUITE AN EFFECTIVE WEAPON, THOUGH. EVEN AFTER IT HAS BEEN PULLED FROM YOUR BODY AND YOU LAY DYING, MUSCLES SURROUNDING THE VENOM SACK CONTINUE PUMPING VENOM INTO THE ANIMAL YOU STUNG.

PPFHT. SOME WEAPON. LOST IN THE WILD AND THE ONLY THING I HAVE FOR DEFENDING MYSELF IS LETHAL TO ME IF I USE IT.

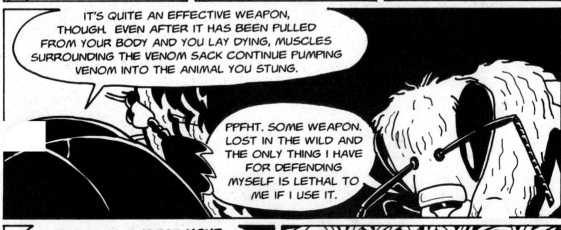

THE STING ISN'T FOR *YOUR* DEFENSE, YOUNG LADY. IT'S FOR YOU TO USE IN DEFENDING THE *HIVE*.

YOU AREN'T THE CENTER OF THE UNIVERSE, Y'KNOW.

YOU'RE PART OF A LARGER COMMUNITY.

OKAY, *OKAY*.

THANKS FOR TELLING ME THAT, SISYPHUS. I OWE YOU. YOU'VE SAVED ME *TWICE*, NOW.

YOU'RE WELCOME. BUT LIKE I TOLD THOM, THE FIRST SAVE WAS AN ACCIDENT.

SO IF IT HADN'T BEEN FOR YOUR ROTTEN DRIVING, YOU WOULDA LET HIM *EAT* ME!?

OF COURSE. THOM ISN'T A VILLAIN, NYUKI. WE MAY DO THINGS DIFFERENTLY, BUT THAT DOESN'T MAKE MY WAY ANY BETTER THAN HIS. WE BOTH PLAY A ROLE IN THE BALANCE OF THINGS AND I WILL NOT INTERFERE WITH HIS ATTEMPTS TO SURVIVE.

BUT---

I THINK THE BIRD IS GONE. LET'S GO.

YOU'LL HAVE TO WALK UP TOP.

ON THE *DUNG?!?*

I KNOW THE GENERAL DIRECTION TO YOUR SWARM CLUSTER, BUT I PUSH BACKWARDS. IF YOU'RE UP TOP YOU CAN TELL ME WHEN WE'RE CLOSE AND HELP ME TO AVOID BUMPING INTO THINGS.

UGH. OKAY.

SO, SISYPHUS, HOW COME YOU KNOW SO MUCH ABOUT BEES?

SIMPLE. THIS WORLD BELONGS TO BEETLES. OUR SPECIES OUTNUMBER THOSE OF BIRDS AND MAMMALS COMBINED AND WE COMPRISE A THIRD OF ALL INSECT SPECIES. I KNOW SO MUCH BECAUSE BEETLES ARE *EVERYWHERE,* WE SEE *EVERYTHING* AND WE GOSSIP.

SISYPHUS?

YES?

YOU'RE GIVIN' ME THE CREEPS.

BWAH HA HA *HAAAAAAA!*

STOP THAT!

YOU REALIZE, OF COURSE, I WAS WORRIED SICK ABOUT YOU.

IT WON'T HAPPEN AGAIN.

I LEARNED A VALUABLE LESSON TODAY, DVORAH.

OH, REALLY?

YEP. THE WORLD IS A *HORRIBLE*, SCARY PLACE.

I WILL *NEVER* GO OUT INTO THAT CRAZINESS AGAIN!

WHAT---? DON'T BE RIDICULOUS.

THE WORLD IS A *GREAT* PLACE. YOU JUST HAVE TO BE CAREFUL.

BESIDES, WHEN YOU BECOME A FORAGER YOU'LL LEAVE THE HIVE EVERY DAY TO COLLECT NECTAR AND POLLEN.

NOPE. TOO DANGEROUS.

THERE'S RISK IN LIVING, NYUKI. YOU CAN'T *HIDE* FROM THAT IN THE NEW HIVE.

MAYBE NOT, DVORAH, BUT I'M GONNA TRY.

SIGH.

WHY AM I NOT SURPRISED?

Chapter Four
HOMEFRONT

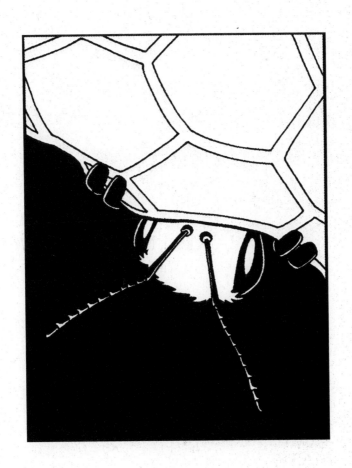

89

93

94

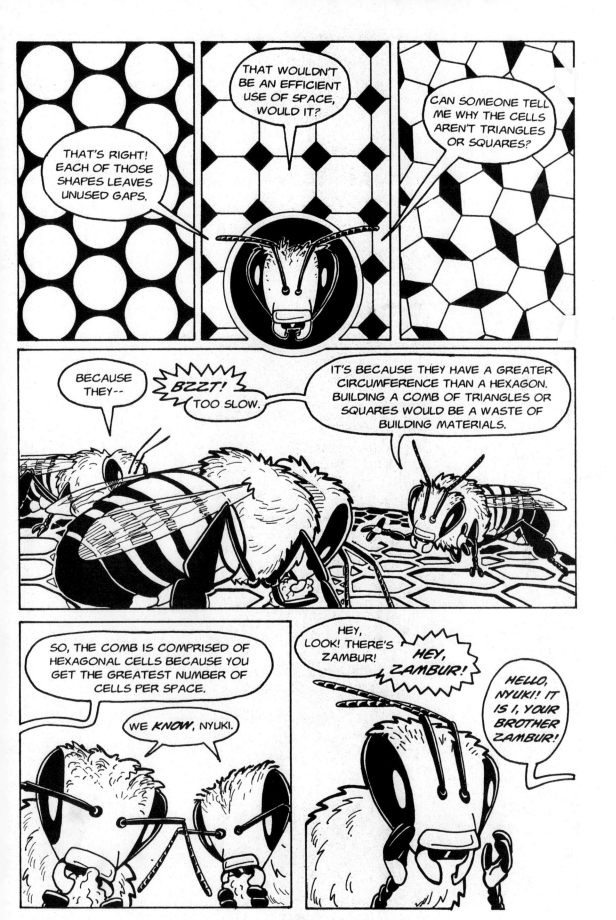

HEY, BIG Z, DID YOU KNOW WE LIVE EVERYDAY ON A STRUCTURE BUILT FROM OUR OWN GLANDULAR SECRETIONS?

HA HA! YOU ARE FULL OF SUCH *WHIMSY*, LITTLE ONE.

I'M *SERIOUS*. THE HONEYCOMB IS MADE FROM WAX THAT WE SECRETE FROM WAX GLANDS IN OUR ABDOMENS

HA! SILLY SISTER, ZAMBUR DOES NOT HAVE A WAX GLAND.

DRONES DON'T HAVE 'EM.

OH.

SEE?

I JUST SECRETED A LITTLE FLAKE OF WAX.

GLORIOUS!

NOW I CAN MIX IT WITH SALIVA AND KNEAD IT INTO SHAPE WITH MY MANDIBLES.

ASTOUNDING!

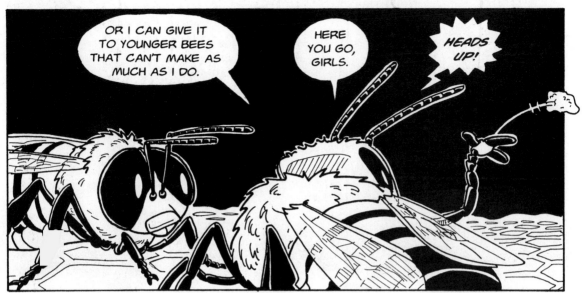

OR I CAN GIVE IT TO YOUNGER BEES THAT CAN'T MAKE AS MUCH AS I DO.

HERE YOU GO, GIRLS.

HEADS UP!

GAH!

BONK!

SHE'S *REALLY* DRIVING ME CRAZY, ARI.

WELL, Y'KNOW, BIJ, I'VE HEARD THAT OUR STING DOESN'T GET STUCK IN INSECTS LIKE IT DOES IN OTHER ANIMALS.

REALLY?

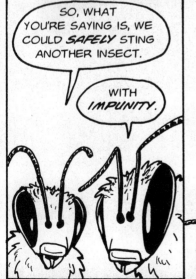

SO, WHAT YOU'RE SAYING IS, WE COULD *SAFELY* STING ANOTHER INSECT.

WITH *IMPUNITY.*

WE BETTER NOT.

YEAH, WELL, I'M JUST *SAYING...*

UM.... ZAMBUR IS HUNGRY, LITTLE ONE. DO YOU HAVE ANY HONEY IN YOUR STOMACH TO REGURGITATE?

I GUESS.

SHEESH. WHEN WILL YOU DRONES LEARN TO TAKE CARE OF YOURSELVES?

I DO NOT KNOW.

WHAT DO YOU NEED THIS FOR ANYWAY?

ZAMBUR IS GOING OUT!

OOO. DO TELL. WHERE ARE YOU GOING?

AH, IT IS A GLORIOUS TALE, BUT ZAMBUR FEARS IT MAY BE TOO THRILLING FOR YOU.

OH, C'MON, TELL ME

AS YOU WISH, SISTER! HEED MY WORDS AND BRACE YOURSELF FOR...

...ZAMBUR'S TALE!

EACH MORN, I, ZAMBUR, LEAVE THE HIVE ON A GREAT QUEST: TO FIND A MATE!

I JOIN MY FELLOW DRONES HIGH IN THE AIR ABOVE A CLEARING IN THE FOREST FOR THE GREAT GATHERING. THERE WE CIRCLE AND SWIRL AND SWIRL AND CIRCLE AS WE WAIT FOR THE ARRIVAL OF A NEW QUEEN.

AND, LO, HER ENTRANCE IS *GLORIOUS!* SHE WEARS THE POWERFUL *PERFUME* OF LOVE THAT FUELS OUR DESIRE TO MATE AND SENDS US ALL INTO A PASSIONATE *FRENZY!*

WE ALL VALIANTLY VIE FOR HER ATTENTION, FOR SHE WILL ONLY VISIT THE GREAT GATHERING ONCE IN HER LIFE AND OF THE HUNDREDS OF DRONES THAT GATHER, SHE WILL ACCEPT ONLY 10-15 FOR MATES.

EACH DRONE SHE CHOOSES WILL COUPLE WITH HER AND GIVE TO HER A GENETIC GIFT WHICH SHE SHALL STORE AND USE TO FERTILIZE HER EGGS IN THE YEARS TO COME. THE DIVERSITY OF HER MATES WILL GIVE VARIETY TO HER YOUNG AND KEEP HER HIVE STRONG.

AND THEN, WHEN THE TIME OF COUPLING IS FINISHED AND THE MALE HAS IMPARTED HIS MATING GIFT, HE BREAKS OFF FROM THE QUEEN AND FALLS DEAD ON THE FOREST FLOOR BELOW!

IT IS A MAGNIFICENT DEATH!

I JUST GAVE YOU HONEY SO YOU CAN GO CRUISING FOR CHICKS?

YES!

AND IF YOU HOOK-UP WITH A QUEEN IT WILL BE FATAL?

MOST DEFINITELY!

GIVE IT BACK.

WHAT?

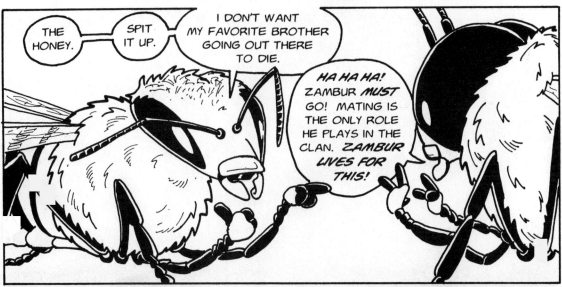

THE HONEY.

SPIT IT UP.

I DON'T WANT MY FAVORITE BROTHER GOING OUT THERE TO DIE.

HA HA HA! ZAMBUR MUST GO! MATING IS THE ONLY ROLE HE PLAYS IN THE CLAN. ZAMBUR LIVES FOR THIS!

YOU LIVE TO DIE?

I LIVE TO DIE SO THAT THE CLAN MAY LIVE.

THAT'S ABSURD.

THAT IS LIFE.

OH-HO, *VERY* DEEP, ZAMBUR.

JUST STAY IN THE HIVE, OKAY?

ZAMBUR?

NUTS.

WELL, I GUESS IT'S BACK TO THE OL' GRINDSTONE, EH, LADIES?

THERE GOES OUR PEACE AND QUIET.

IT NEVER LASTS LONG ENOUGH.

NOW, WHY DO WE BUILD THE CELLS POINTING UP AT A 13% ANGLE?

BECAUSE WE DON'T---

BZZT. TOO SLOW.

IT'S BECAUSE WE DON'T WANT THE HONEY TO SPILL OUT.

WE *KNOW*, NYUKI!

YOU'VE REGALED US WITH THE WONDERS OF COMB CONSTRUCTION EVERY DAY FOR THE LAST 4 DAYS.

I'M JUST TRYING TO CONVINCE YOU OF HOW IMPORTANT THIS JOB IS.

OH, *REALLY*? IT SOUNDS MORE LIKE YOU'RE TRYING TO CONVINCE YOURSELF.

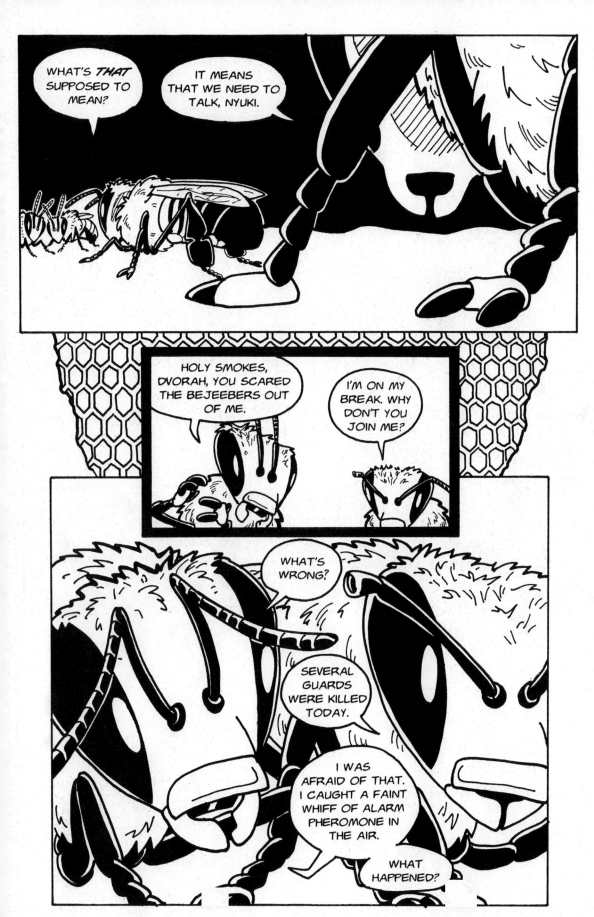

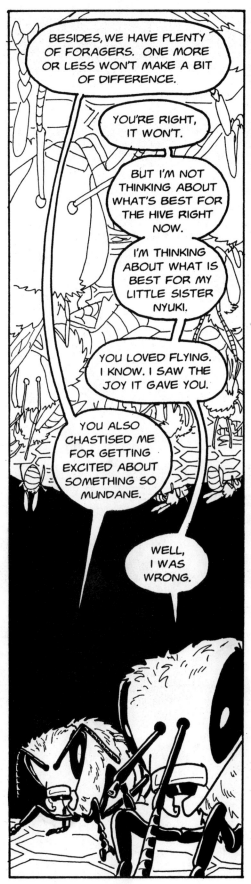

BESIDES, WE HAVE PLENTY OF FORAGERS. ONE MORE OR LESS WON'T MAKE A BIT OF DIFFERENCE.

YOU'RE RIGHT, IT WON'T.

BUT I'M NOT THINKING ABOUT WHAT'S BEST FOR THE HIVE RIGHT NOW.

I'M THINKING ABOUT WHAT IS BEST FOR MY LITTLE SISTER NYUKI.

YOU LOVED FLYING. I KNOW. I SAW THE JOY IT GAVE YOU.

YOU ALSO CHASTISED ME FOR GETTING EXCITED ABOUT SOMETHING SO MUNDANE.

WELL, I WAS WRONG.

LOOK, NYUKI, YOU ONCE SAID THAT YOUR INNER VOICE WAS TELLING YOU TO "GO FORTH TO ADVENTURE!"

DO YOU REALLY THINK IT MEANT PUTZING AROUND THE HIVE ANNOYING YOUR SISTERS?

I DON'T CARE!

NOTHING IS GETTING ME OUT OF THIS HIVE, DVORAH. AND THAT IS FINAL!

BOOM BOOM BOOM

YIPE!

GAH!

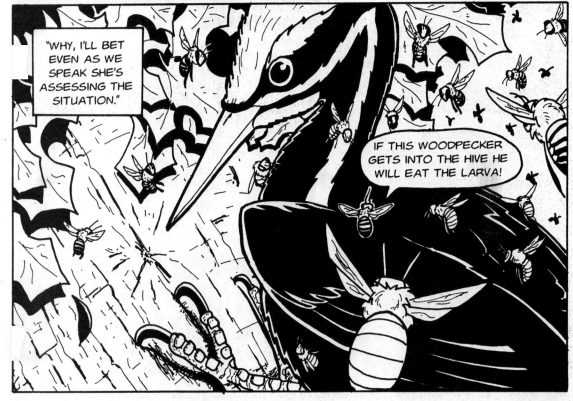

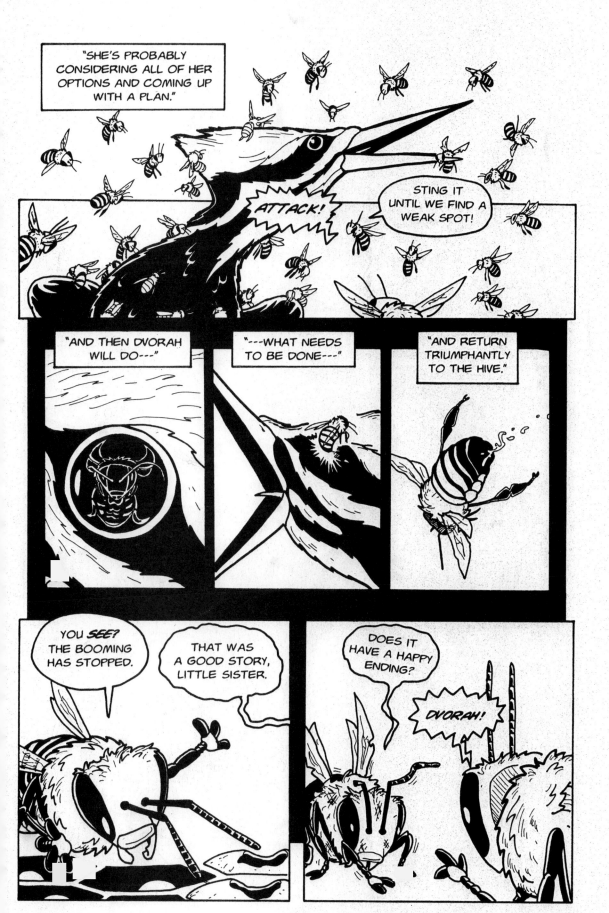

108

SHOO. IT'S *BRIGHT.*

IT'S BEAUTIFUL---

I CAN'T BELIEVE YOU'RE----

I'M *AFRAID,* DVORAH.

YOU'RE AFRAID? *I'M* THE ONE THAT'S DYING.

AND I'M THE ONE THAT IS BEING LEFT BEHIND.

WELL, YOU CAN COME WITH ME IF YOU REALLY *WANT* TO, BUT I HAVE TO WARN YOU IT HURTS LIKE *HECK.*

I'M *SERIOUS.*

YOU'RE MY BEST FRIEND. WHAT AM I GOING TO DO WITHOUT YOU?

Y'KNOW, NYUKI, I AM REMINDED OF SOMETHING I SAW ONCE WHEN I WAS AT MY POST AT THE MOUTH OF THE HIVE.

IN THE MIDDLE OF A STORM I NOTICED THIS *LEAF.*

Chapter Five
THE PLAN

116

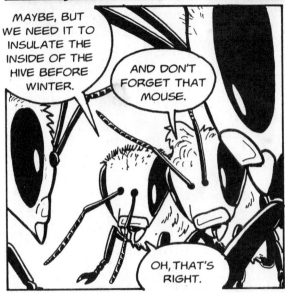

117

IT WAS STUNG TO DEATH BEFORE IT COULD GET OUR HONEY, BUT IT DIED INSIDE THE HIVE.

STUPID RODENT.

SINCE IT'S TOO BIG TO CARRY OUT OF THE HIVE WE NEED TO "EMBALM" IT WITH PROPOLIS SO IT DOESN'T GET ALL NASTY.

STUPID, *STUPID* RODENT.

WELL, I THINK I'M GOING TO KEEP WORKING THE FLOWER PATCH I'VE BEEN VISITING THE LAST FEW DAYS.

THE NECTAR IS GREAT AND I WANT TO VISIT AN OLD FRIEND BEFORE IT DRIES UP.

OKAY. WE'LL GET THE PROPOLIS.

SOUNDS LIKE A PLAN.

EVERYBODY WARM?

I'M ALL TOASTY.

SHALL WE?

LET'S.

NYUKI?

NO WORRIES, GIRLS

WHOOP.

ZIP!

GAH!

I'M OKAY.

118

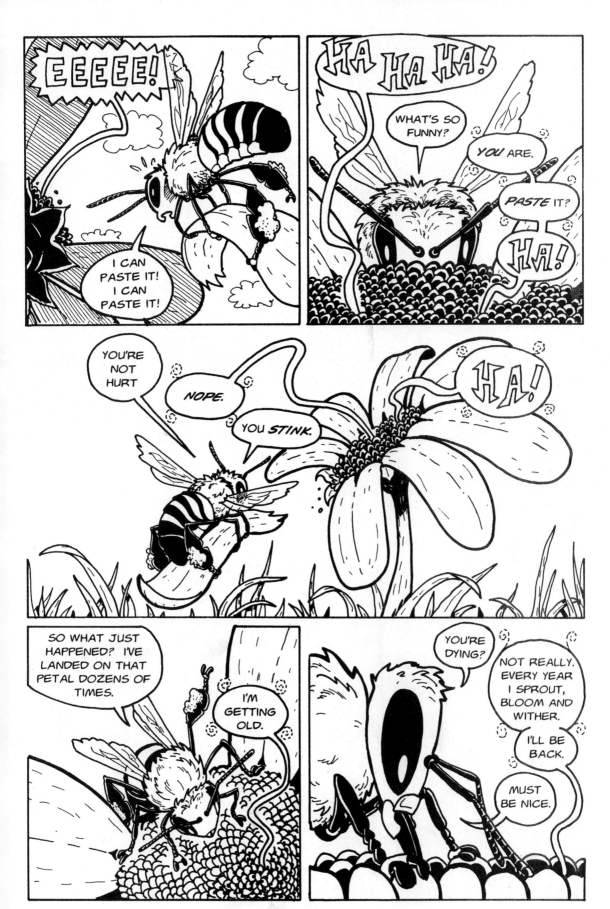

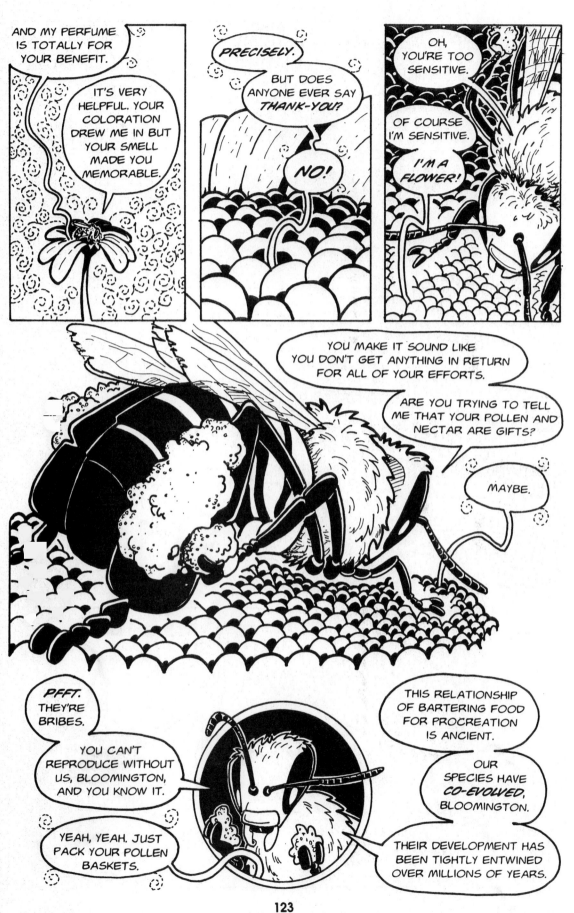

SHE *WAS?*

SHE WANTED ME TO CARRY HER POLLEN TO YOU.

WHAT?!? WELL, GO GET SOME!

NAH.

WHY NOT?!?

BECAUSE I JUST CAME FROM HER.

YOU'RE NOT THE ONLY FLOWER I VISIT.

I'VE BEEN SPREADING HER POLLEN ALL OVER YOU FOR THE LAST FIVE MINUTES.

REALLY?

REALLY?

WHY ELSE DO YOU THINK I'D PUT UP WITH YOUR CRUMMY ATTITUDE FOR SO LONG?

WOO-HOO! I GOT LUCKY!

YOU ARE MY BEST FRIEND EVER, NYUKI!

HA! WE MAKE A GOOD TEAM.

I'VE GOT TO GET BACK TO THE HIVE NOW, BLOOMINGTON.

BE CAREFUL.

I'LL BE BACK.

125

HELLO, MELISSA. I'VE GOT SOME NECTAR FOR YOU TO STORE.

REGURGITATE AWAY, NYUKI.

HOW IS IT OUT THERE?

THINGS ARE DRYING UP. I NEED TO RECRUIT SOME SISTERS TO HELP ME GET WHAT'S LEFT.

I WISH I COULD GO OUT.

YOU'RE TOO YOUNG, MELISSA.

BESIDES, IT'S LATE IN THE SEASON.

I KNOW.

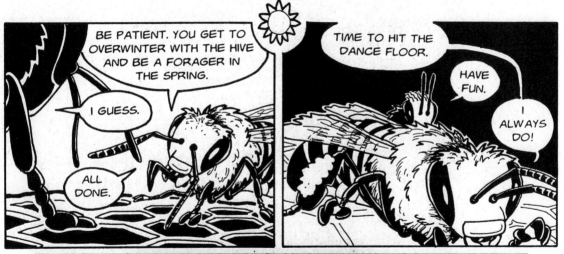

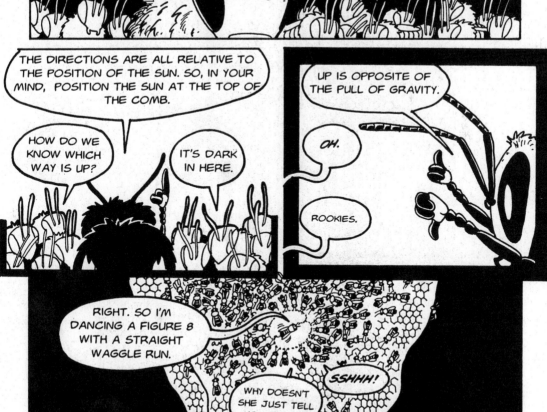

129

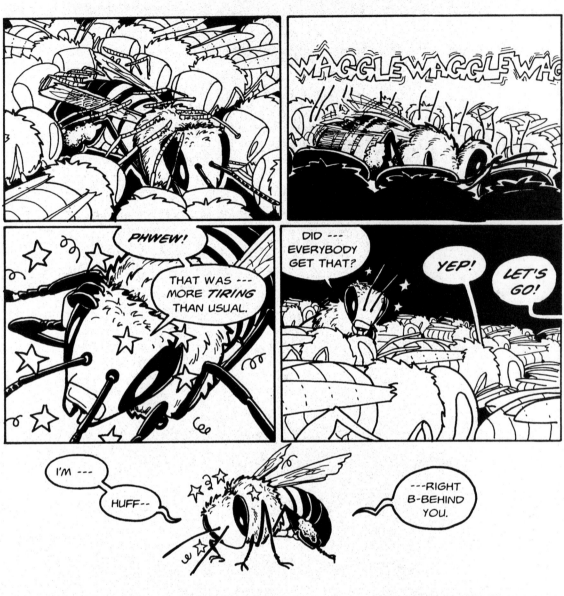

WAGGLEWAGGLEWAG

PHWEW!

THAT WAS --- MORE *TIRING* THAN USUAL.

DID --- EVERYBODY GET THAT?

YEP!

LET'S GO!

I'M ---

HUFF--

---RIGHT B-BEHIND YOU.

NYUK!!

MELISSA?

YOU---UH--- NEVER EMPTIED YOUR POLLEN BASKETS.

NUTS, I'M GETTING FORGETFUL.

WHY DON'T YOU REST AWHILE?

NO CAN DO. I'M ON A MISSION.

C'MON, TAKE A BREAK.

Y'KNOW, I WAS TRYING TO REMEMBER THAT BIG BLOOM STORY YOU ONCE TOLD ME. HOW DID THAT GO AGAIN?

MELISSA.

WHY DO I GET THE FEELING YOU'RE TRYING TO KEEP ME IN THE HIVE?

WHAT? WHY WOULD I DO THAT?

YOU TELL ME.

IF YOU GO OUT THERE NOW YOU MIGHT NOT COME BACK.

OH, YOU WORRY TOO MUCH

I INTEND TO RETURN WITH A FULL LOAD OF NECTAR.

BUT WHAT IF YOU DON'T?

THEN I'M GONNA MISS THIS PLACE.

A LOT.

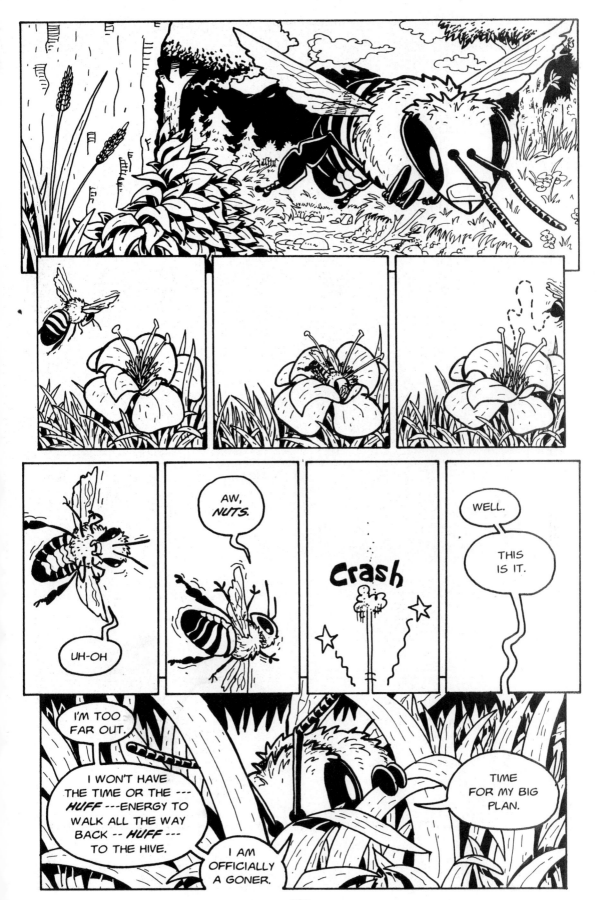

135

136

137

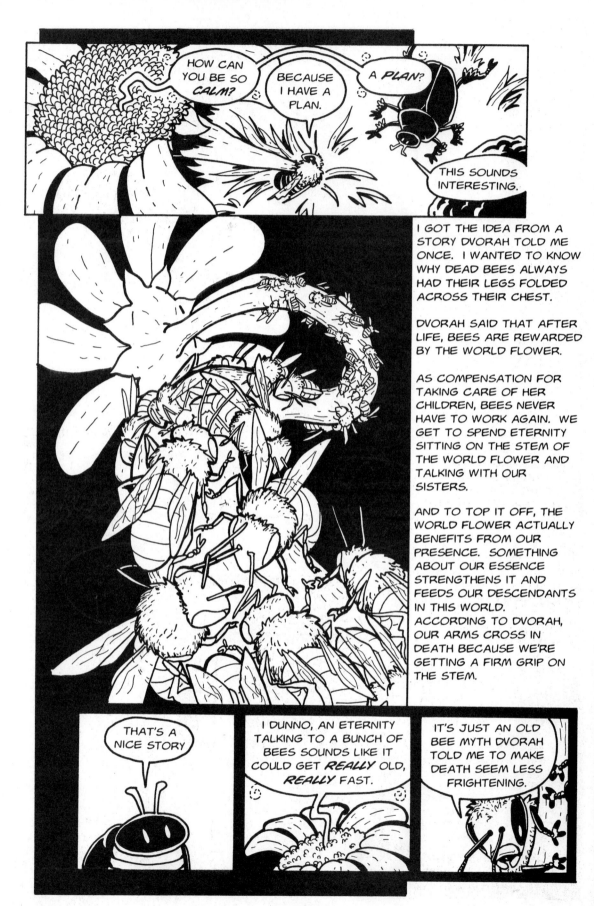

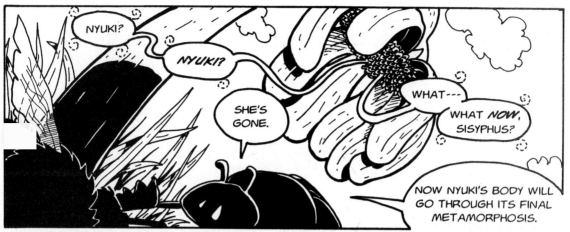

NYUKI?

NYUKI?

SHE'S GONE.

WHAT--- WHAT *NOW*, SISYPHUS?

NOW NYUKI'S BODY WILL GO THROUGH ITS FINAL METAMORPHOSIS.

"THE SEASONS WILL CHANGE, YOUR FLOWER WILL WILT AND HER BODY WILL BE BROKEN DOWN BIT BY BIT BY AN INVISIBLE KINGDOM OF BACTERIA."

"HER PARTS WILL RETURN TO THE SOIL WHERE THEY WILL FEED YOUR ROOTS IN THE SPRING."

"WHAT WAS ONCE NYUKI WILL BECOME PART OF YOUR NEW FLOWER."

"BY THE TIME YOU BLOOM NEXT YEAR, I THINK YOU WILL UNDERSTAND HER PLAN."

AHHH. I *LOVE* THE SPRING.

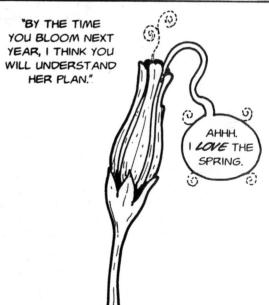

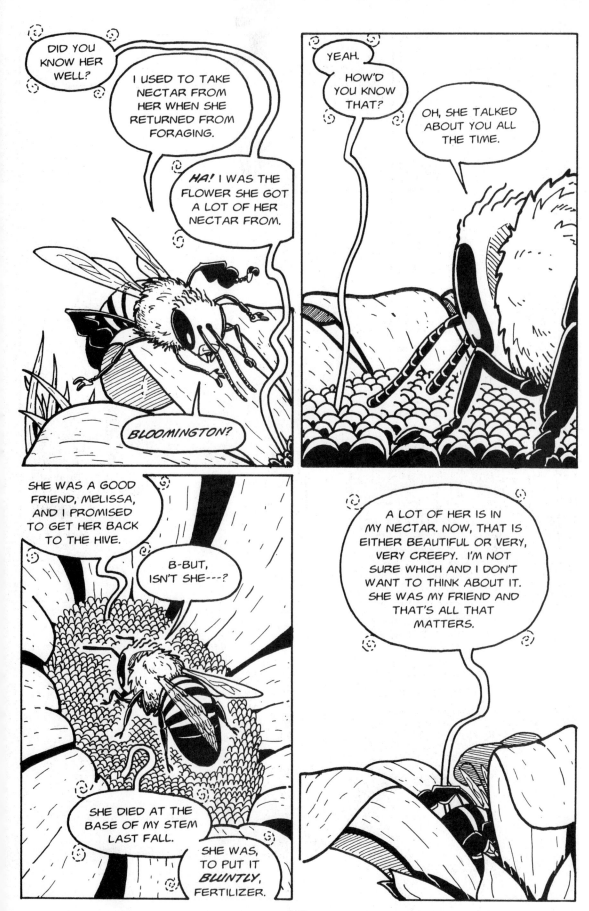

SHE TOLD ME THAT SHE NEEDED MY HELP. SHE PLANNED ON RETURNING TO THE HIVE WITH A FULL LOAD OF NECTAR.

SHE TOLD ME THE SAME THING

AT FIRST, I THOUGHT SHE INTENDED TO BE *CARRYING* THE NECTAR.

OF COURSE, THAT DIDN'T MAKE ANY SENSE SINCE SHE WAS GONNA BE *DEAD*.

BUT NYUKI HAD FIGURED OUT THE CYCLE OF THINGS.

WHEN SHE SAID SHE WOULD RETURN WITH A FULL LOAD OF NECTAR, SHE MEANT THE NECTAR WOULD BE CARRYING *HER*.

THAT WAS HER BIG PLAN TO MAKE IT BACK TO THE HIVE.

CAN YOU GET HER THE REST OF THE WAY, MELISSA?

ABSOLUTELY!

I'LL LEAVE RIGHT NOW.

YOU'RE A GOOD KID, MELISSA.

144

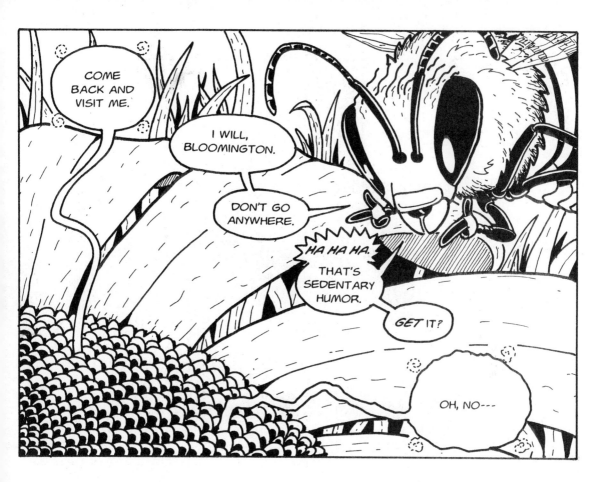

THE END

Bee Lines

Odds and ends from the world of Clan Apis

Insects, insects everywhere While there are anywhere from 1 to 5 million species of insects, Clan Apis focuses on just one species: the honey bee. Insects and their relatives comprise more than 80% of all the organisms in the world. Their small size, quick reproduction and ability to adapt to numerous different environments make them our chief competitors for resources.

Landlubbers Insects were masters of the air long before the Wright brothers and were living underwater eons before Jules Verne created Captain Nemo. But, to be fair, insects had a head start on us. The first fossil evidence of their hexapod ancestors (hexa = six, pod = feet) suggest they crawled onto land over 400 million years ago. That means insects and their relatives were on land adapting to new and different environments 30-40 million years

before our ancestors crawled out of the sea and 100s of millions of years before humans showed up.

Clan Apis *Apis* is Latin for bee. The formal name of the honey bee is *Apis mellifera* and it means "honey-bearing bee" in Latin. This is an important distinction because honey bees aren't the only bees in the world. There are solitary bees and social bees, mason bees, carpenter bees and leaf cutting bees, bees that collect oils and bees that collect pollen and nectar. There are bees that sting, bees that don't and bees that spray acid.

Cave bees Cave paintings indicate that honey bees have been cultivated and raised since prehistoric times.

Can't hold a candle to 'em Next time you light a candle keep in mind the prodigious amount of wax secretion bees had to do so you could have a little illumination.

Where are all the Monster Bees? How come bees don't get as big as you and me? Well, it all comes down to skeletons and breathing. We have our skeleton on the inside and it can support a lot of weight. Bees (and insects in general) have their skeletons on the outside. This exoskeleton (exo = outer) is hard shell made of a substance called chitin and even though it is pretty tough, it couldn't support too much bodyweight.

The other thing that limits an insect's size is how it breathes. In our lungs our blood picks up oxygen and carries it to all the cells in the body. Bees and insects don't have lungs. Oxygen comes into their bodies through little breathing tubes called tracheae. These tubes must branch to almost every cell in the bee's body. If the bee got too big, there would have to be tons of tracheae and oxygen still probably wouldn't get to all of the cells.

Alien Invasion The honey bee that we know and love is not a native of North America. It was an alien species introduced by European settlers for beekeeping hundreds of years ago. By tagging along with the European immigrants, *Apis mellifera* has achieved worldwide distribution.

How to build a bee Like all insects, honey bees have three basic parts: the head, the thorax and the abdomen.

The head contains the brain and much of the bee's sensory apparatus. The bee's antennae are two feelers that extend out from its face. They are used for taste, smell and touch. The eyes are on either side of the bee's head and each is composed of about 6900 facets. Each facet receives a little bit of light independently and contributes one "pixel" to the image that is formed in the bee's brain. The mouthparts are also on the head. This includes the bee's proboscis, which it uses to suck up nectar and water.

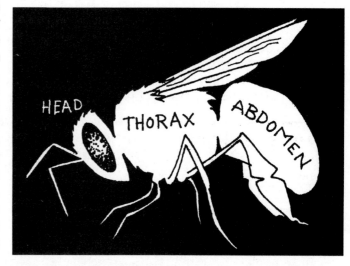

The thorax is the transportation center for the bee. This is where the four wings and six legs attach. The inside of the thorax is full of the very large muscles that beat the wings.

The abdomen is where you find most of the bee's guts. It is comprised of seven external segments. Each segment is made up of overlapping dorsal and ventral plates. A thin membrane connects each plate to the next and allows the abdomen to expand when the crop is full. The crop, or honey stomach, sits at the front of the abdomen. This is where the bee stores all of the nectar it collects from different flowers. There are also the organs that the bee uses to digest its food, excrete its waste and secrete various chemicals. And, of course, in workers and queens, the abdomen is where the sting and poison sac are found.

Bee farm Honey bees pollinate 80% of the agricultural crops in the United States.

A caste of three In the honey bee hive, there are three types (or castes) of bees. The vast majority of bees in a hive are workers like Nyuki and Dvorah and they do almost all of the important work. Workers clean cells, cap brood cells, tend to the brood, tend to the queen, receive nectar from incoming foragers, handle pollen that foragers bring in, build the honeycomb, clean the hive, ventilate the hive, guard the hive and forage for pollen, nectar, water and propolis. All workers are sterile females so they can't

lay eggs. They are also all sisters since they all have the same mother: the queen.

There is only one queen in every hive. She's bigger than her daughter workers and is responsible for laying all of the eggs. The queen leaves the hive only once early in her life to mate. When she does, she will mate with as many as 17 drones and store the their sperm for the rest of her life. When she lays

an egg, she can control whether or not she fertilizes it with sperm. If she fertilizes an egg it grows into a worker or a new queen. When she lays an unfertilized egg it grows into a male called a drone. Since a drone develops from an unfertilized egg, it doesn't have a father. But it does have a grandpa (the queen's dad).

There are only a few drones in the hive relative to workers and, as we saw from Zambur, they look very different from their sisters. Drones have bigger bodies, no sting and enormous eyes that spread all over their head. And they don't do much around the hive. In fact, the workers have to take care of the drones since they don't take very good care of themselves. A drone's only job is mating with new queens.

You are what you eat A fertilized egg that is fed lightly on brood food (a mixture of honey, pollen and glandular secretion from the nurse bees) will grow into a worker bee. To make a queen, nurse bees feed larvae from a fertilized egg large amounts of royal jelly. Royal jelly contains a much higher concentration of glandular secretions than regular brood food. Queen larvae also get fed more often.

Waiting for a butt As we saw in the story, when Nyuki was a larva she spent most of her time eating and eating and eating some more. When the time came to build her cocoon, she used her own feces in the construction. But what kept her from excreting her poop earlier in development? Well, she couldn't. A honey bee larva doesn't grow an anus until very late in its development. So she just had to hold it.

A microprocessor in their heads Bees have 950,000 nerve cells in a brain that is only 1 cubic millimeter in size!

The Calm before the Swarm (no, really)

Nyuki wasn't just making another dumb joke when she made a silly play on the phrase "calm before the storm." The hive really does get strangely quiet a few hours before swarming. Spooky, huh? And then when the hive is ready to swarm, the waves of activity rippling across the hive rapidly crescendo. The bees get more and more worked up as they prepare to swarm until they literally fall out of the hive carrying the helpless queen with them.

Do your own thing Honey bees go through a series of jobs in the hive, but there are no set rules about who does what. While on average most bees follow a general series of jobs starting with cleaning cells and culminating in foraging, bees aren't programmed robots. They can skip around doing different jobs based on the needs of the hive or continue to do one job for their entire life.

Bee Wars You may be wondering why Dvorah and her fellow guards took such extreme action against a bee that was trying to rob their hive. Well, it turns out that one of the fiercest predators that honey bees face is other honey bees. In fact, the behavior that guards display at the hive entrance has evolved primarily to protect their hive from members of their own species. Robbing usually only occurs when there is a dearth of nectar in the field. In fact, when resources are plentiful bees from other colonies are often admitted and adopted into a hive. But when things are bad, foraging bees may seek out honey stores in other hives. They are attracted to the smell of honey coming from a hive entrance. If a robber manages to get past the guards and get a load of honey, she will return to her hive and recruit her sisters to help her plunder the other hive. The resulting conflict can lead to a bee war that may leave thousands of bees dead. The robber bee at the beginning of Chapter Four was darker than Dvorah and the other guards because robber honey bees tend to become smooth, polished and black after multiple fights with other bees.

Smokin' Beekeepers puff smoke into the beehive to make the bees think the hive is on fire. When they smell the smoke, bees fill up with honey before it's all lost. Which is good for the beekeeper, since it's hard for a bee to sting with a full belly.

Why the eye? When the hive was under attack, Dvorah stung the bird in the eye and helped drive it off. But why the eye? Well, when bees get into attack mode one of the things they zero in on to sting is dark colors, just like that bird's big black pupil. Bees are also induced to sting by animal scents and sudden movements.

The sweet kiss Bees often exchange honey or nectar using a process called tropholaxis. Tropholaxis can take place three ways: between workers (as when Nyuki gave Melissa the nectar she had collected), between workers and the queen (workers freed the queen) and between workers and drones (just like when Nyuki gave Zambur some honey to go on his mating flight). During tropholaxis, a worker regurgitates the nectar or honey in its crop out through its proboscis and onto

the waiting proboscis of another bee. Queens rarely feed themselves and receive most of their food from workers. Drones depend on workers to feed them for the first week or so after they emerge but can take care of themselves after that. Knowing this, Zambur must be less than a week old since he is still taking honey from Nyuki.

Tropholaxis is also important during the waggle dance. Dancing foragers will often stop dancing and give their sisters a taste of the nectar they have found.

Workaholic The prodigious queen bee can lay up to 1500 eggs in a single day!

A big, stinky world
Approximately the first half of a bee's life is spent in the pitch-dark hive. Without any light, they can't see a thing but they get along just fine using their antennae. Bees use odors to identify their hivemates and strangers, dancers

transmit the odor of the flowers they visit to dance attendants and queens use pheromone odors to control and direct the activities of the workers. At the mouth of the hive, bees release volatile pheromones to signal alarm. And out in the field, foraging honey bees remember good flowers based on their perfume and mark good flower patches and water sources with a scent they emit. Bees live in a world of odors and their ability to smell (olfaction) may be their most important sense.

A bee by any other name...
All of the bee names in *Clan Apis* are the word for "bee" in different languages.

Nyuki is Swahili for bee. This name was brought to my attention by colleague Sharoni Shafir and I thought it was the perfect name for my heroine.

Dvorah is Hebrew for bee and I also credit Sharoni (a native of Israel) for telling me about this one.

Hachi is Japanese for bee. I thank my friend Harry Itagaki for this one.

Zambur is Farsi for bee.

Abeja is Spanish for bee.

Melissa is Greek for bee. John Wenzel brought this name to my attention but I thought it was a little too common to use. However, by the time I got to the last chapter I had decided that I loved it. Go figure.

Sisyphus the dung beetle was named after that mythological fellow who was condemned to the futile task of rolling a ball up a hill. This name springs from my past as a graduate student. I was in an insect quiz game and my team was asked what the Sisyphus beetle does. I was the first to give the correct answer. Since that happens so rarely, the experience really stuck with me.

Bloomington is named after the hometown of the world's greatest college basketball team.

Acknowledgements

First and foremost let me thank my wife **Lisa** for all of her support and guidance in the production of this book. Lisa had to endure countless readings of initial scripts as I hashed out the events of Nyuki's life. She was always the first (and sometimes the only) person to see the story and art as they evolved. She assumed her role as unofficial editor without protest and was always honest with me (sometimes brutally so). But when I made her laugh (or once, cry) I knew that I was moving in the right direction. We didn't always agree on things, but her proximity to me and the work was vital for its creation. In many ways, Clan Apis would not be the story it is if not for Lisa (so, if you thought it stunk, blame her).

As some of you may or may not know, *Clan Apis* first appeared as a five-issue comic book series. I am deeply appreciative of the financial support **Peter Laird** and the Xeric Foundation gave the first issue of *Clan Apis*. Without their help, I couldn't have afforded to get the ball rolling. For more information about the **Xeric Foundation** you can visit their web site at www.xericfoundation.com

The printing of this volume was funded by my publishing partner **Daryn Guarino**. One couldn't ask for a better business partner: smart, savvy, and able to kick butt at the drop of a hat. Thanks also go out to **Gib Bickel** (co-owner with Daryn of the Laughing Ogre - easily the greatest comic shop in the world), **K.C. Engelman**, **Rod Phillips**, **Harold Buchholz**, **Jim Ottaviani**, **Sue Cobey**, **Brian Smith**, **John Wenzel**, **Sharoni Shafir**, **Levi Lawson**, **Jeff Mara**, **Satish Chandra**, **Harry Itagaki**, **Stan Sakai**, **Leah Itagaki**, **Paul Chadwick**, **Sarai Itagaki**, **Elizabeth Bickel**, **Tara Tallan**, **Wendy Guerra**, **Adam Guerra**, **Mathew Guerra**, **Austen Julka**, **Mark Crilley**, **Simon Smith**, **Nathan Stegelmann**, **Andrew Stegelmann**, **Samuel Stegelmann**, **Marc Hempel**, **Kurt Stegelmann**, **Grant Stegelmann**, **Seth Stegelmann**, **Kim Field**, **Ken Lemons**, **Toni Thordarson**, **Kim Preney** and **Kevin Johnson.**

Bibliography

I have used the following books as reference for *Clan Apis*. I recommend them all to those who wish to do further reading. They also contain several photographs and diagrams that served as valuable visual reference when I was designing the characters and settings.

The Biology of the Honey Bee by Mark Winston
Insects and Flowers by Friedrich G. Barth
The Wisdom of the Hive by Thomas D. Seeley
The Dance Language and Orientation of Bees by Karl von Frisch
A Year of Bees by Sue Hubbell
The Honey Bee by James Gould and Carol Grant Gould
Bees of the World by Christopher O'Toole and Anthony Raw

Contact If you are an educator interested in using *Clan Apis* in the classroom visit the *Clan Apis* web page at **www.jayhosler.com/clanapis.html** or drop me an email at **ActiveSynapse@hotmail.com**

Killer Bee After I had finished writing and drawing *Clan Apis*, I was stung by a bee. Now, you would think that this wouldn't be a big deal for a biologist that has worked with bees for most of his career. I thought the same thing. I was wrong. The following six page story describes the events following that sting. It originally appeared as a promotional mini-comic for the 1999 Small Press Expo in Bethesda, MD.

Killer Bee

IT HAD BEEN A LONG, TEDIOUS EXPERIMENT AND I WAS TIRED. THE LAB WAS EMPTY AND I WAS READY TO GO HOME. AS I WAS REMOVING THE LAST BEE FROM THE TRAINING STATION I ABSENTMINDEDLY LET MY FINGER BRUSH HER ABDOMEN. SHE REACTED SWIFTLY AND PREDICTABLY.

I HAD BEEN STUNG MANY TIMES BEFORE. IT WAS NO BIG DEAL.

WHEN REMOVING A STINGER, IT IS BEST TO BRUSH IT OUT WITH A SIDEWAYS MOVEMENT OF YOUR FINGER. GRABBING IT WILL ONLY INJECT MORE VENOM.

DO

DON'T

SQUIRT

DESPITE THE PAIN, I KEPT MY COOL. I COULDN'T FAULT THE BEE FOR DOING WHAT CAME NATURALLY.

YOU STUPID BEE!

BUT THE PAIN WAS ONLY A PRELUDE.

SOON MY EYES BEGAN TO ITCH, I STARTED TO SNEEZE UNCONTROLLABLY AND MY NASAL PASSAGES SLAMMED SHUT. WHEN I BECAME DISORIENTED, CONFUSED AND WOBBLY I DID THE ONLY SENSIBLE THING TO DO IN SUCH A DEBILITATED STATE.

I GOT INTO MY CAR AND DROVE HOME THROUGH HEAVY TRAFFIC.

I HAB BIN STUNG! I HAB BIN STUNG!

WHERE AM I?

MY WIFE LISA WAS AFRAID THAT I WAS ALLERGIC AND GOING INTO ANAPHYLACTIC SHOCK. I TRIED TO REASSURE HER.

I DINK SWOLLEN TONGUES ARE COMMON DIS DIME OF YEAR, HON.

HOW COULD I BE ALLERGIC TO BEES? I'VE WORKED WITH THEM FOR YEARS.

NEVERTHELESS, WE GOT ONLINE TO GET MORE INFORMATION ON THE SYMPTOMS.

SNEEZING, CONGESTION, DISORIENTATION.

WUDDA COINDIDENCE.

ANAPHYLAXIS IS A WHOLE-BODY FREAK-OUT THAT CAN LEAD TO CIRCULATORY COLLAPSE AND SUFFOCATION IF YOUR THROAT SWELLS SHUT.

FORTUNATELY FOR ME, IT DIDN'T COME TO THAT

THE NEXT DAY I MADE AN APPOINTMENT TO SEE MY DOCTOR. HE PRESCRIBED AN EPIPEN AND INSTRUCTED ME ON ITS PROPER USE.

EN GUARD, YOU STUPID BEES!

THATS NOT A TOY, DR. HOSLER.

I KNOW THAT.

THAT'S NOT A TOY, DR. HOSLER.

SAYS YOU.

THE EPINEPHERINE AN EPIPEN INJECTS HELPS KEEP YOUR AIRWAYS OPEN AND YOUR HEART BEATING IF YOU'RE STUNG.

AHH, THAT'S THE STUFF.

THE ALLERGIST I VISITED SAID THERE WAS A 95% CHANCE THAT MY *NEXT* STING WOULD BE MY *LAST*. HE SUGGESTED I GO THROUGH RAPID DESENSITIZATION THERAPY.

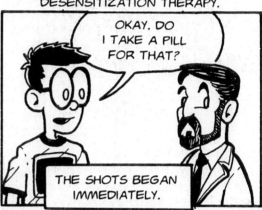

OKAY. DO I TAKE A PILL FOR THAT?

THE SHOTS BEGAN IMMEDIATELY.

TO TEST *HOW* ALLERGIC I WAS, THEY INJECTED ME WITH INCREASINGLY CONCENTRATED DOSES OF VARIOUS INSECT VENOMS AND THEN CHECKED MY RESPONSE TO EACH AFTER ABOUT 5-10 MINUTES.

APPARENTLY THERE WAS A SLIGHT REACTION TO THE LOWEST CONCENTRATION OF BEE VENOM.

OH DEAR GOD!...UH...I MEAN, WOULD YOU LOOK AT THAT?

MY BOSS TOLD ME NOT TO DO ANY EXPERIMENTS UNTIL I WAS THROUGH WITH THE DESENSITIZATION THERAPY. SO, I STAYED AT HOME AND WORKED ON A PAPER I PLANNED TO SUBMIT TO THE *JOURNAL OF NEUROSCIENCE METHODS*.

LUCY! YOU GOT SOME 'SPLAINING TO DO....

ACCORDING TO MY ALLERGIST, A LOW FREQUENCY OF STINGS CAN MYSTERIOUSLY LEAD TO A BEE STING ALLERGY. THIS IS WHAT HAPPENED TO ME. I'M ALLERGIC BECAUSE I HAVEN'T BEEN STUNG *ENOUGH!*

DESENSITIZATION REMEDIES THAT WITH A SERIES OF VENOM SHOTS THAT INCREASE IN CONCENTRATION AND VOLUME, GIVING YOUR BODY A CHANCE TO SLOWLY GET USED TO THE VENOM

SO, BEE VENOM COULD BE LETHAL TO ME.

POSSIBLY.

AND YOU'RE GONNA INJECT ME WITH IT.

OH YES.

AFTER EACH SHOT IN THE ARM, I SAT IN A ROOM AND WAITED FOR A REACTION.

IF YOU SURVIVE THE NEXT 20 MINUTES, WE'LL GIVE YOU THE NEXT SHOT.

THEY STOPPED WHEN I REACTED TO THE FOURTEENTH VENOM SHOT AND TOLD ME TO COME BACK ON TUESDAY FOR THE REST OF THE SERIES. NOT SURPRISINGLY, THE SWELLING IN MY ARMS WAS PRETTY INTENSE THAT NIGHT. THEY HURT LIKE HECK BUT HAD ONE UNEXPECTED SIDE EFFECT.

I FINISHED THE SECOND SERIES OF INJECTIONS AND REACHED MY MAINTENANCE LEVEL WITHOUT INCIDENT. NOW I GET A SYRINGE FULL OF UNDILUTED BEE VENOM (THE EQUIVALENT OF 100 BEE STINGS) ONCE A MONTH. I'M NO LONGER REACTING TO THE VENOM.

157